M000007039

Graceful Last Chapters

Helping Seniors Who Need More Care

Graceful Last Chapters: Helping Seniors Who Need More Care

ISBN: 978-1-68222-066-5

© 2015 C.N. Martindale

All rights reserved. This book or any portion thereof may not be reproduced or used in any manner whatsoever without the express written permission of the publisher except for the use of brief quotations in a book review.

Cover art by Bonnie O'Neal Neher, Professional Fine Art Photographer and owner of Harmony House Studio, Harrisburg, PA. "The Journey", an Archival Digital Image, was shot in the Ranthambore Jungle, India, in 2013. Bonnie has exhibited & sold photographs nationally and internationally. She had works published in books, magazines and a documentary.

Website: www.harmonyhousestudio.com

Email: bneher1@verizon.net

For Gary and Adam, my heroes.
With love, always.

ACKNOWLEDGMENTS

First, a special thank you to my parents for showing me how to live and love with integrity, purpose, and happiness; I'm so blessed to have traveled with you, and I hope this book makes you smile. To all the seniors and their family members who became my friends, I'm proud to have worked with you toward smooth and successful transitions; if you read about an oddly named person with a similar but different set of circumstances than yours, know it's because you inspired me. I miss you all but am grateful for our time together. To Bonnie O'Neal Neher, my intrepid sister-in-law, love and a grateful heart for your perfect cover photo illustrating the crooked road we caregivers walk. To my family and close friends, thank you for always being my cheerleaders, encouraging me, and coming to my rescue in times of need; individually and as a group, you're all a girl could ever want. A special thanks to my editor, Allison, whose eyes are sharper than mine; you shepherded me with a gentle but insistent stick and lots of praise. Any remaining errors are mine, not hers. And lastly listed but first in my heart, Gary and Adam: I could only keep smiling through the last twenty years and complete this book with you beside me, every step of the way.

CONTENTS

PREFACE

You and I have something in common. I have been where you are now—contemplating a long and often complex journey into the world of options for seniors who need more care on behalf of someone dearly loved. Perhaps you haven't yet begun the trip, but you see signs of it approaching. You feel the future beginning to take shape, feel the reality that a journey into difficult discussions and life-altering changes is one you will make and, perhaps, even lead.

We can call what's ahead of you a "trip" or a "journey," but to be perfectly honest, sometimes vocabulary fails us, and this is certainly the current state of the senior-living industry as a whole. Sometimes, there is simply no universally accepted way to label quickly what's really happening.

A senior said to me in my office, "Why do you call it 'senior living'? Look around! It's really 'senior dying.'" Another senior questioned my use of the word "community," as in a residential or senior community. "This place isn't a 'community.' My community is . . ." and then she told me the name of her hometown.

Well, vocabulary isn't perfect, but we do the best we can. Even in writing this book, I can't know who is on your radar due to signs of declining health, so I've had to call the person you read about "your mother," "your father," "Uncle Joe," or even "your loved one." No substituted name is exactly perfect, but sometimes it has to be enough.

Despite that shortcoming, what we're really talking about is an opportunity many of us have to help someone we love craft the best possible way to live, in the best possible place, during their declining years. As you continue to read, understand that what you're really searching for is maximum safety, services, choices, and as much potential happiness as is possible in a home-like environment for a loved one who is only wishing to turn back time. No one wants to become a person with declining health and decreased abilities, changes that make life's pleasures difficult or impossible to enjoy. We'll most assuredly feel the same when our time comes. It is an honor to provide help the way you're doing for your loved one, and they're lucky to have you.

Right now, you may not think of what's ahead of you as an honor, and certainly there will be many times in the months and years ahead when the word "honor" is the farthest thing from your mind. After a long day of addressing whatever needs must be met, you'll be too tired to think of much other than trying to relax and fall asleep. As you drift off, you'll more likely think about how your loved one's life is completely intertwined with yours, even how in the darkest of times you struggle to know where your separateness begins and ends. Honor is far from your mind, but you will eventually know it and feel it.

When it became clear to me that this trip into the world of senior-living options would be mine to make for my mom and dad, I thought of it as just another new chapter in my life, one that would be full of interesting new facts, faces, and decisions. I was astonishingly naïve. I thought I could arm myself as I always had, with education, due diligence, carefully prioritized lists, and I'd be fine; however, that is only part of the equation. Careful preparations beautifully support the intellectual side of our natures but do little to aid the emotional side. None of us who make this journey—on behalf of parents, grandparents, spouses, aunts, uncles, siblings, or close friends—comprehends beforehand the emotional exhaustion that will sometimes overtake us during the pursuit of perfect choices.

I was also wrong when I predicted that the journey to help my parents would simply be another chapter in my life. It became much more—clearly a book and not a chapter, but that is the most obvious short answer. Those facts, faces, and decisions anticipated in the mid-1990s at the beginning of my journey turned into my life's passion, an often very satisfying career, and, even now, a deep desire to serve others as they find the answers they're seeking for their aging loved ones. And therein lays one of the biggest surprises of my journey: we never really know what's ahead, do we? There's only a certain amount of planning and organizing we can do. Some things evolve slowly over time, and sometimes life as we know it changes in the blink of an eye.

I'm still an advocate of researching and educating yourself in preparation for taking on something new, but now I know it's possible, even wise, to impose limits. My need was for a level of understanding so I could ask more questions—for instance, not to be the doctor, but to understand the doctor and advocate for my parents if necessary. We all eventually become quite knowledgeable in all sorts of areas we had no intention of ever learning anything about, and this will happen to you as well. For me, when there was a need to know about cardiomyopathy, ascending polyneuropathy, or decubitus ulceration, I learned enough to satisfy my needs. You will find your own comfort level as you help and support your loved one through times of need.

The feelings—being overwhelmed, frustrated, or getting just plain mad—come at different times for different people. The journeys are never the same, but the guideposts and feelings are similar. Family members would come to my office in the senior community where I worked looking for the perfect new "home" for their mom or a perfect little apartment for their uncle. As we got to know each other and they trusted that I understood their situation, their unexpected tears often surprised them. I'd reach for the always-present box of tissue as they all said some version of, "Oh, for heaven's sake . . . why am I doing this? I never cry, what's the matter with me?" And then I'd say, sometimes with a hand on their arm or maybe a hug, "It's okay. Don't worry, we'll get through this."

Maybe you'll be one of the lucky ones who arrive on the far side of this journey calm, cool, dry-eyed, and full of no regrets. Then God bless you: you have greater endurance and more patience than I did with my parents during the ten years I was caregiver for them. But, regardless of how you arrive on the other shore, no matter the condition you're in when the journey has been completed, my intent is to better prepare you to search options for seniors who need more care. You will have a knowledge base on which to proceed. You will be able to dig a little deeper, ask more questions, and judge better for yourself and your loved one whether the information you're given rings true. You'll have resources and approaches to issues that may not pertain right now, but they may become surprisingly relevant at some later point in time. You will be a better guide, partner, and friend to someone you love and whom you will miss terribly when they're no longer on this earth, no longer just a short trip or quick phone call away.

Finally, my wish for each of you is this: when your journey is complete and the person you love has passed away, quiet will eventually surround you. You'll be alone. There will be thoughts and memories floating through your mind, most of them hopefully happy and full of laughter, but inevitably some not. When this time comes and you hear the quiet, my wish is that you call it Peace, that you have no regrets, and that you know deep down in your soul that you did the best you could. It may not have been a perfect journey, but you did your best, and you can hold your head high. That's our goal and my wish for you.

SECTION ONE

Considering Long-Term Care Options

CHAPTER ONE

Who is This Person?

"Who is this person?" is a deceptively simple question. It's one that you will ask yourself repeatedly, as it applies to different people in a variety of circumstances during the months and years encompassing your journey. I'm going to ask you to think seriously about this question before you clog your mind with a lot of information. More specifically, who is the person you're going to help? Not the label designating their relationship to you, but their deep character traits backed up with as many scenes from their life as you can recall. You may think this is a ridiculous request, but that piece of knowledge often governs how you help them, what you suggest, and how you suggest options to them. Once you add this question to your repertoire, you'll find yourself revisiting it time and time again.

I have traveled your path as a daughter who helped my own parents navigate the often-rocky road of options and decisions that faced them as their health declined, and much of what I have learned came from my years of playing that role. However, as a director of sales and marketing for senior-living residences, it was my job to secure new residents, to keep our apartments occupied and our revenue high. I am the person who would have shown you our community, matched your loved one's needs to the services we could provide, and helped you determine whether our community was a solid solution to fit your needs. After helping hundreds of families over the years, I can offer an insider's perspective from both sides of the fence. And, finally, I'm a lawyer. It is with experience from all of those points of view that I stress the need for you to inhabit the ways and means of this person you love, to know them nearly as well as you know yourself.

You're not going to change them. They're not suddenly going to become gregarious in a community setting if they've never been one who socializes, and a sunny, cheery apartment won't put consistent pep in their step if that's not their true nature. You may think they've been pretty independent-minded all of their lives, but you believe they'll see that they need assistance throughout the day and gracefully accept the help. No, they won't. You'll reason with them again and again, but there's a very good chance they will remain as independent-minded as they always were—perhaps even more so as they feel their control slipping away—and your dear, sweet aunt will suddenly begin to resemble a very stubborn donkey. Who is this person, you'll wonder.

She's the same person she's always been, just older, more vulnerable, and easily panicked about feeling a loss of power and control over her own life. A tiger doesn't change its stripes. A tiger does go on the defensive, though, just as we all do when things don't feel, sound, or smell quite right. That's the person you'll likely encounter when you feel the time is right to talk about changing "home" as they know it. They don't want to talk about change; you do.

You need to talk because you're starting to worry about nutrition, safety, laundry, the bills not being paid or being paid twice, that odd fall that happened during the night's bathroom excursion or while standing at the closet choosing the day's clothing, or mistakes being made occasionally with medication. You try to offer help. "Would you like for me to set up your medication?" But it goes nowhere: "We're fine. We've been doing this forever; we know what we're doing." Or, after repeatedly seeing soiled spots on their clothes, which they continue to wear over and over again, you ask if you can arrange for someone to help take that responsibility off their plate. You hear, "I've always done our laundry. Why should I pay someone to do what I can do?" You think they feel insulted and defensive. You're probably right.

Every family has a different story, a different road traveled to initiate "The Talk." Yes, that's what we really called it at senior communities where I've worked, as in, "Have you and your siblings had 'The Talk' with your mom yet?" Family answers generally began with a yes or no, quickly followed by a retelling of how miserably attempts failed (frustration, discouragement) or a litany of why they hadn't yet tried (avoidance); then came recaptured scenes of failed family meetings (disagreement, dysfunction), and the sequence ended with a general or particular time when another attempt would be tried (hope, determination). The last part, hope and determination, is critical.

Unless you are one of the lucky ones who steps into this situation of necessary change with everything already finalized—all wishes predetermined and properly recorded, all lines of communication open and effective (and let's face it, that means "The Talk" has already taken place and all parties are on the same page)—then you need to continue discussing how help will be inserted into the equation . . . if not now, then at some later point in time to be guided by certain predetermined benchmarks. In other words, a plan is needed and discussions have to happen. The alternative is crisis management. At that point, change is still doable, but you've lost the luxury of time, and the extra layer of stress brought by fear and time restrictions is enormous.

As readers, your individual situations are complete variations of the same story. No one's story is exactly the same. Yet you have picked up a copy of this book, hoping to find a fresh perspective that will help you with your own situation. Each one of you has a relationship that binds you to someone—by blood, time, love, a sense of responsibility, or a combination of these things—and what you need to know for certain is that all of you reading this book have one thing in common: time is moving quickly. For the aging person you love, life's joys and pleasures are decreasing while (at least for you) moments of concern and fear are increasing.

You believe it's time to insert yourself more directly to help, assist, offer a new perspective, and discuss what's happening . . . but how to do it? You first need to take time to fully the answer the question, "Who is this person?" and understand the value of having "The Talk" . . . over and over if the situation calls for it, but sticking with it until decisions are made, agreement is reached, and a plan is created. Yes, there are difficult topics. And yes, there are the difficult topics that no one wants to touch. But you have to go there and trudge through everything, even the topics that are really hard.

That said, don't feel discouraged. This book provides real examples of people and situations that may be similar to yours, while giving insight and support on how you can approach difficult situations. Just know that you, and your loved ones, are not alone.

CHAPTER TWO

The Surprise

It sounds pretty easy to truly understand who your loved one is, proceed with steps to manage an agreed-upon plan, and follow through all stages to the end. But there are many ways it can and often does fall apart. Understanding who this person is includes who they are now, today, and respecting all of it as long as the decisions make sense. You want to keep your loved one safe, yet you also want to be certain all changes to "home" remain within the overall framework of what you know about them. It requires ongoing vigilance, questioning, lots of respectful love, and active determination.

The saddest example I can give you of family managing a plan for their parents is one of not managing it at all—coming so close, but never taking control to execute the plan before it blows up in their faces. It deals with an elderly couple in which the father was diagnosed with dementia, and it's an example of how having a plan that's not fully developed can go completely awry.

Daughter Helen came to me with her mind all but decided: her grandmother had passed away in our Memory Care community several years before, and Helen had only positive memories of the care and compassion Grandma and the family had received. All things being the same now, Helen—who represented herself as Power of Attorney (both health care and finance) for her mother and father—wanted her parents to reside with us upon their eminent return to the area from their condo, which was up for sale in Florida. Her mother was "very with it," though she was increasingly exhausted from caring for her husband. Her dad's dementia was increasing and, as a result, so was the demand on her mother's time as she addressed his needs. He was not a wander-risk, but she needed more help with him throughout the day than she could cobble together on her own. From what Helen described, it appeared her parents could fit within the assisted-living framework unless, or until, the Memory Care community on our campus became the more appropriate setting for her dad.

The plan was that Helen and her siblings would travel to Florida to finish packing up their parents' condo; she would then fly with her parents to Chicago in one week and settle them in their new home with us. All family members were in agreement, and airline tickets had been purchased for travel. We made plans to complete both parents' nursing evaluations, which the community needed to establish their care plans prior to their arrival. Nurses from one of our Florida sister communities agreed to evaluate them in the comfort and convenience of their own condo, then fax us the results.

Helen happily selected the perfect one-bedroom assisted-living apartment and held it in their name with a standard deposit. Family members who were not making the Florida trip would be in touch with me to arrange moving in furniture and decorating the new apartment prior to Helen's parents' arrival, all in the hopes of delighting and surprising them. What could go wrong, right?

When Helen and her siblings arrived in Florida, they found Mom in the waiting room at the hospital. Following an apparent stroke, her dad had been taken by ambulance to the Emergency Room at the local hospital and had just been moved to the Intensive Care Unit. Tests would continue to determine the extent of damage, but clearly the timetable for a move was suspended for some period of time. After several weeks in the hospital and extensive in-patient rehabilitation, her dad recovered nicely, though everyone noted that his previously diagnosed dementia seemed to have been propelled forward by the event. He was noticeably more confused, but he was eventually was discharged back home to the condo with his wife.

What happened next was expected by no one. Helen's mother changed their airline tickets' destination from Chicago to Detroit. The next thing Helen and her siblings knew, their parents were living in, and were determined to remain living in, their Michigan summer house—built as a family getaway years ago during much healthier times and full of happy memories—in the woods by a lake, down winding country roads, "twenty minutes or so" from the nearest small town that didn't have a major hospital. No, they didn't want or need any services coming into the cabin. No, they no longer needed therapy for her dad; they both knew the exercises he should continue performing in order to maintain his strength. Was there a concern about grocery shopping and medical appointments? No, her mom could still drive the car that they had left at the cottage in the garage.

Helen eventually stopped taking my carefully spaced calls to "just check" on her and her parents. She knew that I was concerned about their safety and decision-making capacity, but the family was determined to abide by their parents' decision to live, and likely die, in their summerhouse. I was never able to learn the location of the house, which made it impossible to initiate a call inquiring about interstate coordination of senior services and a possible wellness check to see how things were going with them. It's doubtful that it could have happened anyway without the cooperation and intervention of a physician who knew them and had seen them recently, but it was the only hope I had left.

Losing the nearly filled one-bedroom apartment was totally irrelevant to me, but I pictured my own parents—if they were struggling with the health concerns of Helen's parents, languishing in the "cabin in the woods"— and my mind was filled with only disastrous possibilities. Whatever sub-category of dementia caused Helen's father's suffering, it was supposedly worse than the days before his hospitalization. Given that dementia is a progressive disease and will only worsen as time marches on, what about the risk of wandering now, perhaps off to or into the lake? What about their location being so far from medical help? What about the (exhausted) wife being completely responsible for them both with no reprieve or assistance?

In retrospect, I wonder whether Helen's plan to help her mother and father was truly decided with the parents' full input, or whether it was what the siblings believed could be accomplished once they were together in Florida packing up the condo. Had the Michigan house been discussed and ruled out as a viable option for present-day health concerns? Or was it the folks' underlying hope, one that was avoided and not brought to light? My money's on the latter, though I have no proof and never will. For some odd reason, I envision the parents thinking that they could somehow turn back time by returning to their summerhouse. The Michigan house could have simply been the nine-hundred-pound gorilla in the room that no one would go near.

Lessons learned? Never underestimate the power of determination, which, in some cases, apparently neither diminishes nor improves in its wisdom as people age. Ask the tough questions. Approach and exhaust the gorilla in the room that no one wants to go near, but don't set up the situation for surprise or failure by not talking about everything. And if plans carefully constructed for the wellbeing of your loved ones begin to go south due to events outside your control, still do what you can: move the furniture, take back the airline tickets to use for another time, and put in safety measures—people who will help them and communicate with you during times of transition. Above all, don't disappear for weeks or months at a time, not knowing what's going on, and questioning over and over, "Who are these people?" They're people you love who are making pretty unfortunate decisions. Be there to help execute plans already decided.

In case you're wondering about legalities in this case, perhaps because you find yourself involved with a person or two of mixed decision-making capabilities, it's likely that nothing illegal occurred. As long as one of the parties, in this case presumably the mother, is the competent adult in charge, then they can make their own decisions. Were they the safest, most logical decisions? On the surface, probably not. I never saw the actual Power of Attorney papers that reportedly put the daughter in charge of health care and financial decisions for them both—if indeed the paperwork had been completed. But I would bet the "agent" designation went like this: the mother became her husband's agent when he could no longer make competent choices, and it would not be until the mother became incompetent that daughter Helen would be in charge.

Meanwhile, instead of less attention, there are times when more involvement in family happenings is called for to keep things on track. Is it expensive to fly here and there, take time off from work, pack and unpack, hire help, and chase down answers? Absolutely, it is expensive to the wallet and to the soul. Do you sometimes not want to do what you feel you should do? Right again. It often helps, though, to ask yourself if you're doing the best that you can do . . . just like at your real work, your job. Because, even when your relationship with the person you love is on the top end of the all-time-great-relationships' scale, there are times when helping take care of someone else is just plain, hard work.

CHAPTER THREE

Step by Step

There are countless times I have seen family members or close friends successfully lead processes of effective change to a loved one's surroundings, but my favorite example is about a niece helping her ninety-five-year-old uncle. Leigh adored Robert, and he had always been her favorite uncle. As her dad's oldest brother and the only currently surviving one of ten siblings, Robert was her dad's hero, and undoubtedly Leigh absorbed some of that admiration. Still, I can attest that Robert was an incredibly kind, charming, and thoughtful man with a gentle sense of humor who could easily be everyone's "favorite." He mildly complained with a grin that his eyesight and hearing weren't what they used to be, but at ninety-five, he guessed he was doing pretty well.

Robert was a good conversationalist and asked the kind of questions that made people think a little deeper than they had anticipated. He read the New York Times every day, and he never failed to check the stock market and scores for sports. Although he didn't like to talk in detail about his service in World War II, Robert was very patriotic and extremely proud of his wartime years. An avid dancer, he met the love of his life at a Navy dance in San Diego after the war. Their marriage lasted more than sixty years, and he nursed his wife through her final illness at home, which was her choice. A stubborn and proud Italian, he brought the necessary help into the home but never left her side.

When his wife passed away, Robert grieved deeply in their first and only house, surrounded by their extended family and friends who helped him through this difficult time. But gradually, Leigh, who was the Power of Attorney and Executrix for both Robert and his wife, began to talk with Robert about moving on, being around some new people, doing more, being somewhere where meals and transportation were provided for him, and where the maintenance, cleaning, and grocery shopping would all be less bothersome. She met with a great deal of resistance, but she gently persisted. "Uncle Robert," she would say, "we can do better than this. You can be happier."

When Leigh came alone for her scheduled appointment at the assisted-living community where I worked, she had already been through several previous chapters with Robert, gradually instigating and completing an increasing number of adjustments to his home. Each one—home services coming into the house, then more help, then a move to an independent-living retirement community—was difficult but necessary. What impressed me from the beginning was that Leigh took Robert to the limits of his tolerance each time change was needed. It might not be the ideal resolution, maybe not the one that was best for the long term, which, coincidentally, would have also saved him a few eventual moves and saved her time and work, but it was the most he could handle at the time. She knew him inside and out. So when he was at his limit, she believed him, respected his decision, and gladly made the task her own.

I first met Robert when he came to lunch at our assisted-living community to get a visual picture of Leigh's glowing reports and to judge the quality of our food, which, along with the dining room's general ambience, was very important to him. By this point, Leigh and I had talked and toured our community twice, even choosing to focus on a furnished apartment for a month's respite following Robert's upcoming ankle surgery. The logic was that after surgery and a month or so of extensive physical and occupational rehabilitation at a skilled nursing home, Robert would still need continuing therapy and nursing services before achieving the previous level of independence he enjoyed prior to the operation. Additionally, Leigh was hoping that Robert's month with us would function as a trial run, and he would see the benefit of moving permanently to a community where help was available to him around the clock should he need it.

The dining-room experience fortunately passed muster with Robert, and he enjoyed a good lunch. Afterwards, we talked about his biggest concern, and it made me think of so many other seniors I had met over the years with the same idea holding them back. His current apartment in an "independent living" senior community, combined with his pride that he was correctly labeled there, made it difficult to accept the "assisted living" label at our community. He told me quite frankly that he'd been independent for ninety-five years and had no intention of quitting now.

I explained that the goal is always to keep residents as independent as they possibly can be, even when they have scheduled help throughout the day with particular services. If a resident only needs help with medication, then the nursing staff will not invade their privacy to help with toileting, showers, dressing, or any number of other daily tasks they can perform for themselves. The resident will receive only planned services, which can increase or decrease at any time through the nursing director as needs change. In Robert's case with impending ankle surgery, our director of nursing would visit him at the nursing home where he was rehabbing after surgery to monitor closely his progress in mobility, toileting, showering, and dressing. As he got stronger, help and supervision would decrease, both at the nursing home and within the proposed Care Plan's at our community. Our concern would always be his safety in providing whatever help and oversight he required.

Robert agreed the month-long respite was the best way to see whether the community staff truly existed to help only with activities that were difficult, not to make him increasingly dependent on their services. He reluctantly admitted that he would likely need more nursing services than his current community could provide following rehab, but he was certain he would come to us requiring very little help. He was also adamant that he would not remain in assisted living if he grew strong enough to need only help with medication, which, to him, meant independent living covered his needs. I assured him that we were there to help for however long we were needed, but we also planned with Leigh to do everything possible to help shape Robert's attitude about moving in permanently following the month-long respite.

The ankle surgery went well, and Robert was soon discharged from the hospital to a local skilled nursing facility where he would receive physical and occupational therapy twice daily. Meanwhile, I learned more about what was not working for Robert at his current apartment. Independent-living communities for seniors often means truly independent living, especially if the community is a stand-alone residence with no other level of care associated with it on the same property, which was the case in Robert's situation. The facility provides some combination of meals, activities, and transportation for residents, but help with their individual health care needs is beyond its business model.

Robert's community had an outside healthcare agency—a vendor with a solid reputation but not connected in any way to the ownership backing the community—that was present seven days a week, with staff available to deliver contracted services to residents from roughly seven in the morning to seven at night. Because the most popular service was medication management, a nurse was present during those hours to administer doses; however, no agency staff was available during the later evening or early morning hours. The community's administrators were required to live on site and rotate availability during nighttime hours to answer residents' emergency calls. Since the managers were not medically licensed, however, their response was limited to reassuring the troubled resident and calling 911 for help.

In Robert's case, there had been an increasing number of nighttime 911 calls and trips to the emergency room, generally resulting in short-term hospitalization and a return home with no new diagnosis. Luckily, there were no falls or injuries involved, but the pattern was the same: shortness of breath, increased heart rate and blood pressure, some slight disorientation, mild to moderate panic, and a desire to talk. According to the doctors, nurses, and Leigh, Robert was lonely and, more importantly, was seeking reassurance that even though he was alone, he was safe and okay through the night. To them, the anxiety seemed to center around medical help not being available should he need it during the latter half of the day.

It was Leigh's hope that the logic in 24/7 assisted living staffing during Robert's respite would reassure him, cut down on midnight calls to her, and minimize or eliminate trips to the emergency room for everyone concerned. All in all, the permanent move to our assisted-living community—via the month-long respite trial—seemed like a solid fit on many levels. Leigh remained true to her inherent pattern of informing Robert and helping him feel in control of his decision-making.

Upon "graduating" from his extensive in-patient rehabilitation services at the local skilled nursing home, Robert moved into our fully furnished respite apartment, which Leigh had made as homey as possible, with several trips worth of personal items from his old apartment. His own clothes, towels, toiletries, pictures, pillows, favorite blankets, and meaningful art objects awaited his arrival. When he arrived in his apartment, he was gracious and appreciative of the work Leigh had done to insure his comfort, and his happiness made her happy.

There were initially some lively discussions involving nursing services and Robert's independent (some might say stubborn) streak, but they settled on heavy doses of supplied supervision rather than active assistance with several activities of daily living. Additionally, since Robert wanted to use his walker and switch to a wheelchair when he got tired, scheduled escort service (roundtrip to the dining room three times a day, roundtrip to therapy twice a day) became a lot more time-consuming for staff than initially planned; simply driving him in a wheelchair would have been much faster. Those adjustments were negligible, though, and a normal part of personalizing the service plan, the end result being that Robert was happy and accepting of the true help he needed when he needed it. He immediately began making friends with residents, staff, and managers alike, while his strength and endurance improved faster than anyone had anticipated.

Through the month-long respite, Robert's ninety-six-year-old girlfriend, Mary, whom he met at the independent-living complex and who lived down the hall from him, visited him daily, generally joining him for lunch and being driven roundtrip by either Leigh or our residents' shuttle bus driver. Mary was another amazing example of determined youthfulness. She moved well with her walker, enjoyed good conversation, dressed smartly, wore makeup, had a stylish haircut, and probably fooled most of the people most of the time. Mary had serious heart trouble, was legally blind, and saw only shadows due to macular degeneration. She and Robert were clearly devoted to each other, and she cheered him greatly, undoubtedly contributing to his speedy recovery and certainly his positive attitude simply by her presence.

Leigh and I carefully timed conversations with Robert and Mary, individually and together, about the possibility that they could both move into our community, not only for the security of around-the-clock assistance but also so they could be together. Perhaps, we thought, they might consider combining their separate apartments into one two-bedroom apartment. As Mary said, they could consider "living in sin." Both practicing Catholics, neither of them took the "sin" part lightly, even at their age and with both of them having been previously married. However, in terms of both time and energy, they spent a significant part of each day navigating space to come together for meals, activities, outings, and simply to spend time together. They felt that since time and energy were likely both in relatively short supply, they wanted to think about living together, so we looked at a couple of options as the month drew to an end. Though they were reluctant to leave their friends in the independent apartment complex, the idea of hosting lunches or dinners in their new home appealed to them, and they went so far as to admit that several of their friends could surely use our services as well. Then something happened that none of us saw coming.

Here's Truth Number One: As you probably already know, if you've been involved to any degree with doctors and seniors, a doctor's word is golden to our elders and is never questioned. It's like God Himself speaking. It's definitely a generational respectfulness, but to our elders, whatever doctors say becomes fact. So when Robert had his final checkup regarding his ankle and the post-surgery rehabilitation, the appointment was with the orthopedic physician who had performed surgery, not his regular doctor who had known him for decades. The surgeon talked with Robert, had him perform several movements, and watched him walk the length of the hall and back on his walker.

After his return trip, the doctor asked Robert, "How do you feel?"

"Great," replied Robert, "I could go several times that distance."

The surgeon then said that he felt Robert was independent enough—there's that word again—to return home. Bingo!

Fortunately, Leigh was present and interjected history about Robert's increasing number of nighttime emergency-room visits and hospitalizations prior to the ankle surgery, and she noted that during the past month with the assisted-living services and availability of night staff, emergency hospitalizations had not been an issue at all. The surgeon thought it sounded like the anxiety problem had resolved itself, but to be certain, he suggested Robert set up an appointment with his own doctor, which they did for the next day.

Here's Truth Number Two: As a professional courtesy, doctors rarely, if ever, overrule each other. When Robert's general practitioner, who had known him for more than thirty years, and who had been intimately involved in the nighttime admissions to the hospital via the emergency room, told Robert he was glad his assisted-living experience was so positive and productive, he also noted that Robert might want to think of moving there permanently sometime down the road. Nevertheless, he concluded, "If your surgeon says you're independent enough to return home, then I have to agree with him." Leigh could hardly get out of Robert's way fast enough to avoid being trampled by him and his walker as he raced out the door. Two doctors, same verdict, done deal.

Robert returned to our community after the appointment and gave notice that he was moving out the next morning. Mary joined him for dinner at the community that evening, and I made one final attempt to recap the positives they had both experienced during the last several weeks with us, including their enthusiasm of sharing an apartment together. It was slightly difficult to keep the list of positives on track, since we were constantly being interrupted by residents and staff saying goodbye, giving hugs, and telling them how much they would be missed . . . all best of intentions, of course, that fell on deaf ears. Robert and Mary were too excited about Robert's success and their new lease on remaining in independent living to have anything assisted-living-related ruin the moment. Robert reminded me that he'd said in the beginning that if he was independent enough after his respite month with us, he would return to independent living rather than stay in assisted living . . . and two doctors said he was ready.

Absolutely: he had warned everyone, and the time was here. We rejoiced in his accomplishments, though poor Leigh was slightly less enthusiastic, having gone through the disappointment of the doctors' appointments and now moving all of Robert's belongings back to his old apartment. She much preferred the thought of moving the remainder of his furniture along with Mary's into the new two-bedroom, but she hid it well, and the entire move-out occurred the next day.

While this may seem like the end of Robert and Mary's story, it is not. Robert happily returned to his independent living arrangement and, while on his walker, fell three times in the first two days back home, the last fall being serious enough to put him in the hospital for a series of tests. Doctors determined that he had had several mini strokes and could no longer live alone. The earlier hospital-rehab assisted-living pattern was repeated, though in a shortened version. After a week or so in the hospital, he returned to the nursing home for two weeks of therapy, and then was discharged to us and his new two-bedroom apartment with Mary waiting.

The weeks in-between were a blur for Leigh as she also helped Mary move. In addition to seeing Robert nearly every day to monitor his progress and also transporting Mary back and forth to the nursing home, she had to clean out two apartments, move and unpack all the items, and decorate the new apartment in a manner that would make it feel like home to them both. She accomplished it perfectly with the help of her husband and some extended family who, without exception, were just as smiling, pleasant, and concerned about Robert and Mary as Leigh herself was throughout the whole process.

Lessons learned? In light of the bigger picture of events transpiring around Robert, this is a small suggestion that still may have had an important impact. When Leigh went with Robert to the second doctor's appointment, she could have minimized the odds of the GP agreeing with the surgeon if she had briefly recapped in writing prior to the appointment her thoughts on exactly WHY it was dangerous to approve a return to independent living. The financial costs of hospital readmissions are an anathema to most doctors and hospitals right now, and combined with a reminder about anxiety being diminished with around-the-clock medical staffing, it might have made a difference. Of course, if Robert had stayed with us instead of returning to his old apartment, a more successful outcome would have depended on our nursing evaluations catching his decline prior to the falls and, secondarily, the optimistic idea that a good argument would be enough to cause Robert's GP to ignore Truth Number Two and overrule his colleague. Still, I urge communication on all fronts, even if it's just a note slipped to the doctor prior to the appointment.

As you can probably tell, I admired Leigh's strength. The way she showed her love and respect for Robert was inspiring: she didn't do things her way or necessarily the easy way. She went to church every morning, and I imagine that her daily talks with God became longer and sometimes more prayerful as she tried to serve her uncle's needs, but she never once faltered in her actions. She sometimes disagreed with him, and she never failed to put all of the cards on the table during each and every hand. It's just that she respected it was Robert's life in question, and she was there to help him. Naturally, if Robert had been failing mentally through this process and not making sound decisions, her response would have been necessarily different. But you have to remember that he was doing everything right, absolutely following doctors' orders, and striving to do the best he could do to accomplish his goals . . . which he did exactly.

At every moment, Leigh knew the answer to Who Is This Person? It mattered who Robert had always been, as well as who he was at that moment, and she allowed him to be as independent-minded as he could be safely. She also knew Mary. For Mary, it wasn't at all about the labels of "independent" versus "assisted," but instead it was how to remain with Robert for as long as she could, as easily as she could, that trumped her reservations about leaving the friends they enjoyed together. She didn't want to move any more than Robert did, but she wanted to be with him, and she wanted them to have the care they needed to make their time together the best that it could be.

Mary, too, was very independent-minded. She verified more than once that it was permissible to bring in her own healthcare aide multiple times each week rather than use our services and staff, and despite her virtual blindness, she insisted on signing her full legal name countless times on our more than one-hundred-page lease. Having been in banking her entire life, she knew an "X" would suffice as her signature, but she would write her name as long as she could. Proud and admittedly stubborn, Mary was really all about loving Robert, and that not only bound her to Leigh but also became a part of Mary that Leigh honored.

Doing the right thing is not always the same as doing it the way we, as caregivers, want to or the way we think is right or easiest. It's their life, their final chapter to write. There's no denying that choosing to help facilitate the chapter's action is exhausting, exasperating, and at times seemingly endless, but it is also honorable service that can eventually bring peace and closure. Whether or not you face the number of chapters that Leigh faced as you help facilitate the changing levels of care needed by your loved one, you have an example of how your first resolution may not last forever. Time passes and needs change. By all means celebrate and enjoy the new life and solutions you've helped bring to their lives, but stay alert. The crystal ball we all wish we had available to us simply doesn't exist.

SECTION TWO

Caregiving Challenges

CHAPTER FOUR

Who Are We?

When I had the opportunity to help my parents through their later years, I was just as unknowing and as naïve as anyone else—just like you, just like all of us. This isn't a personal failing of any kind: it's just that when you are at the center of your own event, you sometimes lose the ability to see the bigger picture clearly. You're so caught up in putting one foot in front of the other to get through the day. You can learn from my experience and be better prepared for what will become part of your life.

My parents' move to be near me was due to Dad's deteriorating health from an extremely bad fall and, as a result, Mom's feelings of being increasingly overwhelmed with his care. It's not that he was always at home and dependent on her care alone; he was cycling in and out of hospitals, rehab centers, then home, then starting over, and each time accumulating new diagnoses, doctors, specialists, therapists, visiting nurses and aides. At this point in time, they were both in their mid-eighties and had been completely independent prior to Dad's fall—driving, shopping, going to concerts and plays, involved in church and social activities, and enjoying a large circle of friends. But like many couples of that generation, one was the leader and actually did most of the instigating and facilitating, while the other played a crucial support role. Mom's was the support role.

She had never consistently done grocery shopping alone, never routinely paid the bills, and certainly never dealt single-handedly with the world of hospitals, healthcare providers, accumulating medical bills, and getting herself where she needed to be by driving alone. In fact, Mom didn't even learn how to drive until her mid-forties, when she took a full-time teaching job and I started kindergarten. We were from a small town in Indiana, and after living there for more than thirty years, they knew everyone and everyone knew them. Retirement was an exciting adventure for Mom and Dad . . . to move to a place they chose for its beauty, to meet new people, to learn the winding roads and find their way around the beautiful foothills of North Carolina . . . until Mom had to do it alone.

My two older brothers and I were scattered—Minneapolis, Harrisburg, and Chicago—but we burned up the telephone lines and tried to help long distance the best we could as their health, especially Dad's, declined. I was in law school at the time, and I can't remember a set of finals that I went into without wondering if my airline flights would get me to North Carolina in time to be truly helpful at the moment of need. Sometimes Dad was in a hospital; other times he was in rehab or back at home. Since we had had "The Talk" several times over the years, we continued to have shortened mini-versions over the phone and face to face when I was there. But we nevertheless held onto the original agreement through this difficult stage: they would let us "kids" know when they needed our help. One time when Dad was back in their apartment with Mom, they both called and said they had decided it was time to ask for help. I thought I knew what this meant, but I asked Dad to clarify. He said, "We think it's time to move closer to family. We need your help."

My brothers and I had all offered to have them move near us, but I think we all knew I would probably be the logical one who would be chosen. As the youngest by eight and eleven years and the only daughter, I had a little different relationship with Mom and Dad than my brothers did. Plus, there were Illinois connections: Dad was born and raised in a small town in southern Illinois, he and Mom lived in Chicago during their early married years, and they often traveled there to see relatives over the years. In short, it didn't feel quite as foreign to them as either Minneapolis or Harrisburg, and they could almost fool themselves into believing it when they said, "Coming home to the Midwest just felt right."

When we got the word that the move was on, my brothers and I divvied up the tasks in large chunks and worked quickly. Bill (Minneapolis) took care of hiring packers and a mover, then flew to North Carolina to oversee the process, close out accounts, corral medical records for them both, and help Mom stay as calm as possible. Tim (Harrisburg) made the arrangements for Dad, who was back in a nursing home and unable to travel by either car or a commercial plane, to fly by air ambulance from North Carolina to Chicago. Then Tim flew to North Carolina to get the records and legal documents from Bill, check Dad out of the nursing home, and fly with him to Chicago. My job was to get them settled in a senior-living community, which I had been working on for several years—taking my time investigating, learning, discarding, mailing them heavily notated collateral from options that might work, discarding again, until only one choice actually survived.

Their chosen senior-living community not only fit the long and specific list of "must-haves," but it was ten minutes from my house and, they could keep Schatzie, their beloved Schnauzer, which was their number-one non-negotiable item. As soon as summer school ended for me, I flew to North Carolina, picked up Mom, Schatzie, and their car packed with all the items not entrusted to the movers, and we took a road trip to their villa in a newly opened independent- and assisted-living community. We arrived in the Chicago area with a couple of days to spare, which we used to put the finishing touches on their new home before Tim, Dad, and the fabulous folks from the air ambulance company brought us all together. Then the real work began.

I may as well insert right here that there is no such thing as a good move. It can be across the country, across town, or across the hall, and they are all equally bad for seniors. Even though I saw it first with my own parents, I saw countless variations with residents and their families as I worked in senior communities over the years. It makes no difference how much you try to pre-plan and simplify, and it makes no difference how hard you work to make it easy on the person being moved. Even if you do all the real work, it's still work for them just to adjust to the new surroundings, to find the things they need, to feel acclimated to their own things in new space. They become frustrated, agitated, cranky, discouraged, depressed, and totally exhausted from sleep deprivation, all of which can be exacerbated by mental and/or physical impairments or poor health in general. Truly collaborative team efforts from a variety of disciplines can minimize the impact of Relocation Stress Syndrome, also known as Transfer Trauma, but you'll find that those efforts will rarely come together in any meaningful way unless you lead the effort yourself.

The villa was a huge hit with Mom and Dad. Decorated with their furniture, pictures, and special possessions accumulated during more than sixty years of marriage, it immediately looked and felt like home to them both. That turned out to be a huge positive that I used relentlessly— along with how much easier the day to day would seem now that I was there to help—to nudge them into a sense of security.

It's true they were no longer alone. I could and would take over many of the troublesome tasks Dad could no longer do, and I helped in any other way I could as the days unfolded. It's true that their day would be simpler in many ways. For example, dinner could be brought to them from the main building's community kitchen every day, unless Dad felt well enough to go with Mom to the main dining room and meet some of the residents; the plan cut out one meal preparation, reduced the grocery list I said I'd handle, and gave them something to look forward to. It's true their coverage for medical needs was lined up prior to their arrival, which seemed like an expedient thing to do. Dad's new electric wheelchair was delivered hours before he himself arrived; a local doctor was chosen and an appointment scheduled within a few days. Home health was alerted to come evaluate Dad's needs, and the director of nursing who ran assisted living came to see whether or not a care plan was appropriate for either of them. Help was on its way.

The real problem after Mom and Dad arrived, however, was that no one anticipated from the faxed nursing notes just how bad Dad's condition really was. We knew that he had to be classified as independent living to get the services, care, and frequency he would need coming into their home, but the documentation nursing received was abysmal. Apparently, the nurse-to-nurse conversations were not much more revealing. He was very weak, malnourished and terribly thin, dehydrated, and in considerable pain when he was moved; the bedsores (decubitus ulcerations) that were reportedly "red but healing nicely" were really stage two and three out of a possible four stages. Let's just say, I don't think the wounds developed on the flight to Illinois. They either didn't know how to stage the sores, the reporting was grossly negligent, or both. At any rate, the picture given was false.

Wound care became an immediate top priority. He also was unable to shift his position in bed or get out of his bed, unlike we were told, so a hospital bed with an air mattress was ordered and delivered. As an aside, the bed issue was very upsetting to Mom; she understood this was what he needed, but since they had always slept together, the idea of a hospital bed was a psychologically difficult concept. Once he got situated with the new bed, alternating occupational and physical therapists started coming every day. The therapists were concentrating on useful strength, like being able to use the bedrails for mobility in and out of bed and being able to stand and bear weight. These were enormous hurdles for Dad, and his condition was really too weakened for the progress needed. A Hoyer lift was added to get him in and out of bed.

Daily wound care continued, therapists and supply people were in and out, homecare came to bathe and dress him, nursing assistants came to help with toileting, and Mom was trying to get him to drink and eat. Time passed, the doctor made house calls, and some days were better than others. There were days when he was fully dressed and went to the living room via wheelchair to eat and watch TV for a while, and there were other days that he couldn't get out of bed. It seemed like the doorbell was always ringing (and the dog always barking), but the schedule was basically services for getting up and going to bed, some toileting checks throughout the day, then wound-care nurses and therapists coming and going. It was overwhelming. They never made it to the main building's dining room for dinner.

We tried hard to celebrate life's joys and little celebrations. When Dad was positioned correctly in his bed, he could look out his bedroom window and see the large pond that began at the edge of their sloping yard. The day's count of ducks and geese was fun, and the ducks' water skier-like landing on the pond's surface always brought a smile or chuckle. Seeing the two visiting herons pace the pond's perimeter for food was something we looked forward to every day. Dad never made it outside on the back deck to feel the sun on his face, hear the honking of the birds, or toss seed over the rails to watch them gobble it up. Through the ups and downs, however, it was a blessing for my son Adam, who was in middle school at the time, to help brighten their days, do little chores for them, have some good talks, and participate with his dad Gary and me in his grandpa's eighty-sixth birthday in September.

We decorated like we always did for birthdays, with streamers, balloons, cake, presents, and cards. Dad needed considerable help from Mom and me unwrapping his presents and cards, but their many friends, relatives, and our family all came through to note the special day. We tried really hard to keep up the pace, celebrating as much as we could before he got too tired. He was gracious, though, and he enjoyed a small piece of birthday cake before returning to bed when the nurses arrived.

Thanksgiving felt a lot like Dad's birthday; that is, we tried hard to make it look, feel, and smell like our traditional family holiday, but it was really about how he felt and how much he could tolerate. I cooked everything at our house, and then the three of us took all the food to them. Mom had set their dining room table with good china, glassware, and silver. With the centerpiece and Thanksgiving napkins, it could have been a picture from any one of our many years past. There were still the required "oohs" and "aahs" at how good everything looked and smelled, but I'm sure I wasn't the only one missing Dad's triumphant presentation of the beautifully browned turkey on the big china platter reserved especially for the event.

As it turned out, Dad was too weak to get out of bed that day and really couldn't eat very much. Home health and nursing had already been there earlier in the day, but Mom didn't process the negative reports and was weepy at his inability to join us to eat Thanksgiving dinner. She stayed with Adam and his dad Gary to eat buffet-style and watch football on TV, while I took a little plate of soft food choices—mashed potatoes with gravy, a few scraps of tender turkey, and bites of pumpkin pie—into Dad in the bedroom and ate with him in there.

I remember that meal with a very grateful heart. While I fed him and picked at my own plate, we had a good talk, reminiscing about Thanksgivings past, and particularly those we spent joining his relatives in his hometown for the holidays. Those celebrations were much like his growing up years—big family get-togethers of forty to fifty people or more, mounds of food, noisy storytelling, laughter, and rejoicing in their history together. We both needed that time, I think, and were especially thankful for our blessings of having time to spend together.

By Christmas the next month, I had graduated from law school, and Dad was in a nursing home. The shifts of various help coming into the villa had been peeled away one by one, generally with compassion but always firmly. Insurance was declining to pay for services because Dad was not improving, and they could no longer stay to help. His body was failing him. Mom and Dad declined hospice care and, at the same time, declined a live-in caregiver to help with Dad's increasing needs. Hospice, fifteen years ago, was for the imminently dying, and my parents thought that if the hospice label were imposed, Dad would just give up entirely.

Dad said and Mom believed that he wanted to live, that he would try harder, and he would get better. Every day that was a better day than the last, I found myself hoping it was the beginning of an upward trajectory, that it was the start of the time their hopes and prayers would be answered . . . when it was, in fact, just a good day, likely followed by a day or two or three of decline. Of course he wanted to live—we all wanted it—and Mom certainly wanted that more than anything in the world. They both wanted it so much that they couldn't admit he was dying. I remember telling them that their choices were certainly okay, but their decisions backed them into a corner they may not welcome: a nursing home was the only remaining option.

The answer to the question, "Why not have live-in caregivers for your Dad," is pretty simple. As annoying as the constant coming and going of healthcare providers had been—sometimes they were late, or early, or didn't come at all; sometimes they were rude or condescending; sometimes they were messy and didn't clean up after themselves—my parents could not imagine having a stranger live with them permanently. They had always taken care of each other, through thick and thin, and Mom remained fiercely independent and self-reliant even as she struggled to do the simpler tasks among the ever-growing list of daily care. The possibility of turning to a stranger for help in their home was not on their radar. Refusing live-in help, to me, made perfect sense based purely on Mom and Dad's personalities and who they were, individually and as a couple. It was simply not an option without the time it would require to adjust their thinking, to get them out of remembering the way life had always been and move them into the harsh, unrelenting light of today's reality. They could not make the leap in a timely manner.

But hospice was different, and in looking through the rearview mirror at years past, it's the only thing I regret. I've often said that if I knew then what I know now about hospice, I could have somehow helped them to a better decision, but that's not entirely true. Hospice has changed dramatically over the past fifteen years, and their messaging about palliative care is no longer only about the last days of life, though that is still certainly a part of what they can do to be so helpful. The goal is to work with not only the patient but also the family, with hospice providing comfort and preserving dignity in the face of terminal illness. In addition to pain and symptom management, there is equal emphasis on emotional and spiritual support for patients and bereavement support for families. With what there was to work with as the year 2000 approached, however, I can regret my role in not being able to bring Dad the best possible end-of-life experience and to help Mom at the same time with her grieving, but I cannot change what hospice had not yet become.

Even with the choices my parents made, Dad still had an adequate supply of morphine, was lucid when not asleep, and I think for large chunks of time—unless the nurses were turning him in the bed which, at that point had become an exercise of bone scraping on bone—he was without the excruciating pain that was a part of his last months. He had a very strong and healthy heart, which just kept on beating throughout his ordeal, but it finally gave out, and he slipped away in late February. The cause of death was sepsis from the decubitus ulcerations.

After all of this vastly simplified yet lengthy overview of the first six months of caring for my parents, this is the simple thing I want you to learn. Throughout these complicated, often devastating, and extremely busy days, I was asked repeatedly by doctors, nurses, healthcare attendants, therapists, facility managers and staff, well-meaning neighbors up and down the street where Mom and Dad's villa was located, and probably many other categories I now forget, "Are you their caregiver?" "No," I would answer, every time, with an open and honest heart, "I'm just the daughter helping out as best I can."

Well, now I know I was mistaken. The answer should have been, "Yes. Yes, I am." And so are you! If you are doing any number of small, medium, or large tasks that are helpful to someone you love and it consumes some measure of time from your life, then you are a caregiver. I wasn't trying to be cute with my answer or to be someone who consistently tried to "split hairs" as some measure of defiance. Instead, I honestly looked upon myself as a daughter doing what daughters do to help and thought the real caregivers were the professionals coming and going while getting paid for their work.

What's true in that thought process is that the paid professionals are called "caregivers," but don't lose sight for a moment that you, too, are in that same category. You are likely the primary caregiver, one who is neither being paid in monetary remuneration nor is looked upon as a professional, but you are most assuredly counted as one of the millions of people rightfully labeled "caregiver" to which the facts and statistics apply. Why is it so important to realize the label "caregiver" fits daughters, sons, spouses, in-laws, grown grandchildren, friends, and any number of other relationships?

It's the first step in recognizing that you will be changed by the help you're providing to someone you love, and though you may feel alone, you are in excellent company. It's a very large group to which you belong, and there is help that will ease your mind, body, and soul. Please don't do as I did and shove all of the helpful information that's available under the erroneous heading "Take Care of Yourself," which I thought I was doing anyway and, therefore, didn't need to spend more time reading about something I already knew. Please read with an open mind. Learn, adapt, and find comfort in knowing that you are not alone. Try to embrace who you have become.

This quote, by Rosalynn Carter, Former First Lady of the United States (February 1997), speaking as the newly appointed Chair of Last Acts, neatly sums up who we all are.

"One of my colleagues once said, 'There are only four types of people in this world:

Those who have been caregivers;

Those who are currently caregivers.

Those who will be caregivers; and

Those who will need caregivers.'

That seems right to me."

For More Information

Tracy Mintz, "An In-Depth Look: Relocation Stress in Older Adults," OpenPlacement Blog, November 26, 2012, accessed April 8, 2014

https://www.openplacement.com/community <https://www.openplacement.com/community

Rosalynn Carter, "Remarks," Honorary Chair of Last Acts, February 13, 1997

http://gos.sbc.edu/c/carter.html.

www.rosalynncarter.org/about_rci/

Comprehensive caregiver resources, including twenty-two dementia capability webinars (screening tools, legal issues, financial capacity, using technology, determination of need, family conflict, managing problem behaviors). Focus is providing local, state, and national partnerships for effective caregiver supports in health, skills, and resilience through advocacy, education, research, and services.

CHAPTER FIVE

The Impact of Caregiving

For the purposes of this chapter, I am a reporter of facts and statistics that I find somehow strangely comforting and disturbing at the same time. While I'm guessing that most of us know several friends, relatives, or acquaintances that are currently or have been caring for someone elderly, I'm also quite certain that you'll be shocked at the number of people nationwide who are involved in caregiving much like we are. This group of unpaid caregivers to which we belong is not only surprisingly large in size but is also poised to grow exponentially over the next few decades.

The projected growth of our group is due primarily to changing demographics and, more specifically, to the impact of aging Baby Boomers, who started turning age sixty-five in 2011 and who will continue to markedly increase projections of all types for more than twenty years. Simply put, the more people who are aging, the more care and caregivers will be needed. Secondarily, as cost of care in all types of senior-living communities continues to rise annually in comparison to at-home care costs, it seems efforts will continue to be made to keep seniors in their homes as long as possible using both paid and unpaid caregiving services.

In 2010, 40 million seniors age 65 and older accounted for 13 percent of the US population, but this cohort will increase to 72 million (19 percent of the population) by 2030. By 2050, seniors age 85 and older—often called the "oldest of the olds," the group most likely to need long-term care—will grow from 5.5 million in 2010 to 8.7 million in 2030 and to 19 million in 2050. As this group ages and requires help throughout the day to maintain their independence, the number requiring assistance in more than two Activities of Daily Living (ADLs) will increase from approximately 10 million in the year 2000 to about 21 million in 2040. As such, they will need either increased levels of care at home or in a community setting, and the choice for many people often becomes a financial decision.

In 2014, the national median cost for a private room in a nursing home was $87,600 a year ($7,300 per month), while the median cost of a private one-bedroom apartment at an assisted-living facility was $42,000 annually ($3,500 per month). Both care options increased in cost an average of 4 percent per year for the last 3 years.

At the same time, national median hourly rates for home health care aides ($20 hourly, $45,200 annually) and homemaker or companions ($19 hourly, $43, 470) have remained relatively flat, only increasing 1 percent annually during the same timeframe.

Most people pay out-of-pocket for either community or at-home options, with at-home care often augmented through adult day-care centers (national median cost $65 per day, $16,900 per year).

This brings the estimated total private dollars Americans spent on long-term care options in 2013 to more than $211 billion.

Since cost of care is relative to income, however, it's interesting to note that the median cost of nursing home care ($87,600 per year) is 240 percent of the average annual household income of seniors, while in-home care costs average 88 percent of seniors' household income. In stark terms, two-thirds of people age 65 and older do not have sufficient assets to pay privately for even one year of nursing home care.

A study from John Hopkins University Press (2012) estimates that in the United States 85 percent of all help provided to seniors is provided by family members.

In 2013, approximately 15.5 million Americans—unpaid caregivers comprised of family members, other relatives, and friends —provided nearly 17.7 billion hours of care valued at more than $220.2 billion.

The number of caregivers in 2013 increased by 100,000 individuals when compared to 2012, which in turn had increased by 200,000 individuals over 2011.

Similarly, 2013's 17.7 billion unpaid hours of service increased by 200 million more hours than in 2012, which had increased 100 million hours over 2011.

The estimated value of unpaid hours in 2013 ($220.2 billion) increased $3.8 billion over 2012, which increased $5.9 billion over 2011. (For calculations on how these numbers were obtained, see references in "2014 Alzheimer's Disease: Facts and Figures.")

Finally, please note that while many of us struggle with caring for a loved one with Alzheimer's disease or any of the other related dementias, many of us do not. Those of us who don't are not included in the already staggering numbers provided; therefore, this statistical picture does not begin to cover the full spectrum of what our unpaid hours of caregiving mean in terms of captured data for economic value. Despite the particularity of Alzheimer's disease and other dementias that place useful boundaries and limits on surveys tracking numbers such as these, the result is that there are more of us working for more hours than is currently being calculated.

The effect of the time we give freely to care for loved ones touches much more than the calculation to determine unpaid hours nationally. Friends and family, most often spouses and adult daughters, spend approximately $5,000 each year out-of-pocket on caregiving expenses for a loved one. We also use up personal days at work, vacation and sick time, family time, and even trim work schedules to find the time to do what we need to do. Therefore, we financially jeopardize our own futures through reduced earnings and contributions to our savings. This not only affects our finances and careers but also our lifestyles, relationships, happiness, social lives, personal health, and overall state of mind.

This is who we are, the primary caregivers for someone we love who needs help, and we're willing—without always calculating the long-term effect—to make sacrifices large and small. Realize, though, as the hours and days pass, the effect is cumulative. Stress increases and sleep likely decreases in both amount and quality. We wear ourselves thin, often seemingly trapped in the ubiquitous "Sandwich Generation," unable to choose between giving diminished efforts to either our own children or our aged loved ones. This, too, shall pass. The important thing, perhaps, is to consciously recognize who we are and what we're doing, thereby being able to better care for ourselves along the way. The good news is that we have the blessings of both young and old family members in our lives today, right now, at this moment . . . and it will not always be this way. Someday, the chance to do better will be gone, so let's see how we can help ourselves move wisely through this chapter of life.

For More Information

"Older Americans 2012: Key Indicators of Well Being," AgingStats.gov: Federal Interagency Forum on Aging-Related Statistics, Washington, D.C. 2012

http://www.agingstats.gov/agingstatsdotnet/Main_Site/Data/2012_Documents/Population.aspx.

"Genworth 2014 Cost of Care Survey," Genworth Financial Inc. and National Eldercare Referral Systems, LLC

http://www.genworth.com.

LN Gitlin, R Schultz, "Family caregiving of older adults," in Public Health for an Aging Society, eds. RT Prohaska, LA Anderson, and RH Binstock, (Baltimore, Md.: The John Hopkins University Press, 2012), 181 – 204.

Richard Johnson, Desmond Tochey, and Joshua M. Weiner, "Meeting the Long-Term Care Needs of the Baby Boomers: How Changing Families Will Affect Paid Helpers and Institutions," May 2007

https://urban.org/UploadedPDF/311451_Meeting_Care.pdf.

L. Harris, M. Sengupta, M. Park-Lee, and R. Valverde, "Long-Term Care in the United States: 2013 Overview," National Health Care Statistics Reports, Number 1, Hyattsville, MD: National Center for Health Statistics, 2013

http://www.cdc.gov/nchs/data/nsltcp/long_term_care_services_2013.pdf.

"Evercare Study of Caregivers: What They Spend, What They Sacrifice," National Alliance for Caregiving, November 2007

www.caregiving.org/data/Evercare_NAC_CaregiverCostStudyFINAL20111907.pdf

Naomi Freundlich, "Long-Term Care: What Are the Issues?" Robert Wood Johnson Foundation, February 2014

www.rwjf.org.

"2014 Alzheimer's Disease: Facts and Figures," Alzheimer's Association

https://www.alz.org/alzheimers_disease_facts_and_figures.asp#impact

"Alzheimer's Disease: Facts and Figures," Alzheimer's & Dementia, volume 10, issue 2, Alzheimer's Association

https://www.alz.org/downloads/Facts_Figures_2014.pdf.

"Rising Demand for Long-Term Services and Supports for Elderly People," Congressional Budget Office, June 2013

http://www.cbo.gov/publication/44363.

Linda Barrett, "Caregivers: Life Changes and Coping Strategies," AARP Research, November 2013

www.aarp.org/research/topics/care/info-2014/caregivers-life-changes-and-coping-strategies.html

CHAPTER SIX

Helping Ourselves

It sometimes comforts me to know that what troubles me, troubles others. When I was knee-deep in caregiving responsibilities, I didn't know that as a group, caregivers struggle with many of the same conflicting thoughts that often rolled across my mind. Not only do we all share many similarities as we meet our caregiving demands, but healthcare groups know about us, study us, and document our struggles.

For example, in a 2013 AARP survey studying areas of change in caregivers' lives as compared to life before becoming a caregiver, the reported positives and negatives corroborate the often-competing emotional changes we feel as we become involved in caregiving responsibilities. The study documents that areas of positive change (being pleased to help someone, recognizing a closer relationship with the person helped, and feeling proud and satisfied to be a caregiver) are at war with the negatives (wishing things were different, being fearful of outcomes, feeling others should be more helpful in the caregiving process). This survey represents a snapshot in time of only the participating individuals, but the tension between positive and negative emotions is nearly universal. What this means to us is that if we cannot change the swirl of competing emotions that likely arise, we can still improve the way we deal with it. How much success we have long-term over the changes in our lives depends on our coping skills and how much we help ourselves through periods of transition.

According to the same AARP survey, women who become caregivers tend to cope with mounting stress through prayer or meditation, support from their partners, and contact with a close circle of trusted friends that includes siblings, children, and other healthcare professionals. If indeed these are the known ways we best cope, then we need to maintain and strengthen those activities and relationships. We have to make time for ourselves through some combination of social connection with family and friends, perhaps even meeting new people with similar concerns—if not through a face-to-face support group, then by searching for a legitimate group online. We need support and understanding that comes from open, non-judgmental communication, which takes time, commitment, and some leniency for trial and error. From our individual histories and our own intuition, we know the people, experiences, and situations that support us, and that is what we need to nourish. You know what works for you; you just need to make a plan and use it.

I often wonder why it's so hard to make a plan for myself with me at the center of it. I think for many of us who become caregivers, our natural instinct is to put the needs of others first, which often causes our own wants and needs to languish in the wings, waiting. This time we need to step beyond what comes naturally. As a caregiver, you have to advocate for yourself, be proactive, and become selfish about your time. Taking care of your self is now a necessity and not a luxury. But if you need more clarity, consider this: what happens to your own carefully constructed situation if you don't take care of yourself? If you're taken out of the equation, will everything collapse like a house of cards? No one wants that, most especially the loved one you are caring for.

Our biggest effort needs to be finding time to nurture relationships and maintain activities that make us happiest. That alone will be a huge goal, but if we approach the caregiving demands with eyes open, knowingly and with determination, the pay-off could be enormous. By contrast, if we don't make the personal goal front and center at all times, then caregiving commitments, time, and emotions will combine into a life of its own—swirling, consuming, and powerful. It's the difference between giving control to the demands of caregiving or keeping control for yourself, and it's much healthier to choose the latter in the long haul.

Remember, you're not only making choices for today; you're actually initiating patterns for an unknown number of years full of stressors that have not yet revealed themselves. And therein is the difficulty: we simply cannot know the length of time we'll be in the role of caregiver, what challenges the disease process will bring, or what amount of heartache we'll experience and endure. It is nearly certain, however, that there will be a personal cost to you during the caregiving years, both in terms of the physical and emotional toll it can take, but small steps and consistent effort on your part can minimize the cost.

One simple way you can start taking care of yourself is by scheduling your "time off" as if it were a doctor's appointment or some similarly scheduled commitment, and block off the days and time on your calendar with as much care as you do for everything else. Do you take yoga or exercise classes that you enjoy? Write them on your schedule. Do you see your friends occasionally for a drink or a bite to eat? Make it a regular appointment with a frequency that seems reasonable, and then make some calls to get the first few booked and write them down. If you enjoy family movie night or have a semi-regular date night, then block them off in writing. The point is to give the same care and attention to your own emotional health as you give to others, and writing down a scheduled day and time forces our brain to make more of a commitment than if we leave our best intentions in control. I offer you this suggestion from my own years of caregiving, and I know it would have made a big difference to visually see personal wants on the calendar alongside the musts I considered written in stone. Best of intentions are that and not much more.

We also need to keep ourselves physically healthy (doctors' appointments, diet, exercise) and mentally strong. It's not at all unusual for caregivers to struggle with signs of depression and anxiety, so don't be surprised if you explain symptoms to your doctor and her head is nodding affirmatively before you even complete your sentence. Remember the numbers: 15.5 million Americans providing 17.7 billion hours of unpaid care, and it's estimated that up to 70 percent of those caregivers deal with clinical depression. Healthcare professionals widely use an overarching term to describe what we experience: Caregiver Syndrome or Caregiver Stress Syndrome. It is not yet a formal diagnosis in the Diagnostic and Statistical Manual of Mental Disorders, an American Psychiatric Association publication defining all mental health disorders, but it carries with it a set of recognized symptoms. These include: anxiety, depression, irritability, feeling tired and run-down, difficulty sleeping, overreacting to minor nuisances, new or worsening health problems, trouble concentrating, feeling increasingly resentful, drinking, smoking, or eating more, neglecting responsibilities, cutting back on leisure activities, etc. If you're reading the list and mumbling, "Yep, check, check, yep, got that," then please talk with someone you trust for some help. Friends and family are terrific for support, but healthcare professionals will understand caregiving stresses and point you in the right direction.

Consider hiring someone else to occasionally or regularly perform some of your caregiving tasks. A hired professional might cause a pang or two of guilt and seem like an extravagance at first, but most of us consider them a true godsend and the time their help frees up for us as a gift. I first hired help with Mom's medication management, and it was worth every penny. It became a piece I depended on that returned some normalcy to the mother-daughter relationship, and their presence took away from the fact that I was caring for my mother. Before long, Mom knew details about the aides and their families, and she was even buying birthday cards for their children. They became more like visitors than healthcare aides, which is not to say that she still didn't notice when they were late or didn't complain bitterly when a personnel change occurred. I also saw many good examples of non-nursing helpers assisting our community residents, and good "fits" resulted in long-lasting friendships. The helpers ran errands to the store, drove them to their long-time beauty salon or barber shop, helped with laundry, ironed clothes, helped write notes and send cards to friends. They will do countless little things that free up your time but feel like appreciated attention to your loved one.

Other means of securing breaks from caregiving demands include adult daycare centers and respite services, which you may find to be especially helpful if your loved one is aging at home instead of in a community setting. Good providers of these services are invaluable to tired, stressed caregivers, and can do a very brisk business. I had a daughter of a potential community resident who couldn't say enough good things about the daycare program she found for her mom; in fact, she felt the socialization and activities were helpful enough that she kept her mother enrolled for a while even after she began transitioning into our community. Eventually her mother's ties to her new home became strong enough that she eventually quit the adult daycare program without trouble and spent time exclusively with us.

For good respite services, you will probably have to make a series of phone calls to senior communities in your area, and be forewarned that some of them will have a week's minimum stay. The daily charges may seem prohibitive, but remember there's a cost for twenty-four-hour staffing, even when it's not broken out as a separate charge. Many people use this to cover caregiving concerns when they go on vacation and will be out of town, but others, like Leigh and Robert in chapter 3, use respite as a "trial" of a senior community that will hopefully turn out to be a new, permanent address. Either way, or in combination, a respite stay offers the taxed caregiver a well-deserved and necessary break.

For me, the caregiving years became about trying to exert some degree of control over the things I could control, and there's no surprise that it came at a time when I felt there was so much in my life that was uncontrollable. It helped to focus on things that interested me outside the day-to-day routine, which also seemed to reduce stress because I was doing something for me. One of the biggest positive changes I made was future-oriented, and I made it along with my two brothers.

Mom and Dad had looked seriously at long-term care insurance late in their retirement years but found the premiums to be cost prohibitive, probably due to their ages and pre-existing conditions. When my brothers and I saw what was happening to Mom and Dad's assets as they progressed through the stages of care they needed with only Medicare and supplemental insurance, we began looking into long-term care insurance for ourselves. We began investigating long-term care companies, then got referrals and started interviewing, then chose policies for our spouses and ourselves. Not only were we trying to protect our individual resources in light of what we watched happen to our parents' finances, but we were also putting plans in place to prevent the stress of not planning for the future that will arrive eventually for all of us. We've planned for the care we will need.

Feeling relieved and productive after our policies were secured was reinforced for me by what I saw at my job. In helping seniors and their families in the decision-making process about community retirement living, I routinely managed the cost discussions to help them determine how they were going to pay for the proposed expense in a community.

Looking back, my estimate is that it was prohibitively expensive for more than half of those who were seriously considering community living. The repeated pattern was that they could afford the apartment and the embedded services (rent), both short term and long term, but they could not afford the additional monthly cost of care they needed on top of rent. It was an eye-opener for them that the cost of care would keep increasing as their health declined and they needed additional help.

In these cases, there were all kinds of financial solutions and avenues to explore before giving up, but one truth emerged over the years: very few people in our parents' generation were savvy enough as investors to secure long-term care insurance. For the most part, the biggest investment that held the most hope for financial return was their home. And, of course, when the bottom fell out of the economy and housing values plummeted, it seriously affected options for seniors once they began needing care and a change in "home" as they knew it. All too often I saw cases where options for obtaining care that was needed and wanted was postponed for years because of non-diversified investments. They were still able to make some adjustments, but the number of options decreased considerably while the amount of stress on the family increased greatly.

That was the scenario I tried to prevent for my family and, more directly, for my husband and myself. Even removed from our decision to obtain long-term care insurance by more than a decade, it still feels good to have controlled a significant piece of an unknowable future, and I'm happy that we have not regretted the decision we made. It's an expensive proposition, and it's no wonder that, at best, little more than 10 percent of Americans have long-term care insurance. We acknowledge that we've made sacrifices to maintain our policies, but I believe it can be even more expensive in the long run to do nothing in preparation for a future we know will eventually arrive. It might be something you and yours may want to consider.

When and if the urge to control something in your life strikes during your years as a caregiver, then take a look around for something you feel is a productive option to investigate. I can't say mine was fun . . . and it was an expensive decision, so perhaps you can do a lot better than I did. I think the point is to get some satisfaction, to create change that feels good, and to get outside our day-to-day challenges by planning for something else. It's proactive and feels good, even for a while.

For More Information

Linda Barrett, "Caregivers: Life Changes and Coping Strategies," AARP Research, November 2013

www.aarp.org/research/topics/care/info-2014/caregivers-life-changes-and-coping-strategies.html

"Caring for the Caregiver: How to Find the Balance You Need," ComForcare Home Care Services (blog), May 2013

http://blog.ComForcare.com.

"A Way Forward: Highlights from Beyond Dollars 2013," Genworth Financial, Inc.
https://www.genworth.com/dam/Americas/US/PDFs/Consumer/corporate/Beyond%20Dollars%20FINAL%20109048_093010_secure.pdf.

Andree LeRoy, M.D., "Exhaustion, anger of caregiving get a name," CNNhealth.com, August 13, 2007,

www.cnn.com/2007/HEALTH/conditions/08/13/caregiver.syndrome/index.html

"Caregiver Stress and Burnout: Tips for Recharging and Finding Balance," Helpguide
http://www.helpguide.org/elder/caregiver_stress_burnout.htm.

"Heart Disease and Caregiver Burnout," reviewed by Thomas M. Maddox, M.D., Web MD, May 12, 2012

http://www.webmd.com/heart-disease/heart-disease-recognizing-caregiver-burnout.

Naomi Freundlich, "Long-Term Care: What Are the Issues?" Robert Wood Johnson Foundation, February 2014, www.rwjf.org

https://www.alzheimersspeaks.com.

SECTION THREE

Creating a Plan

CHAPTER SEVEN

It's Time to Talk

You've arrived at the point where you're going to initiate a discussion about long-term care options and planning with your mother, your father, or whoever it is you love and needs help—either now or sometime in the near future. Home, in its current design and how it's been functioning for them, is no longer the optimal care choice. You feel that something has to change. You have been thinking about getting this conversation started for a long time, probably avoiding it, and now you've decided to act. That's a huge step in the right direction! Sometimes anticipation is worse than actually doing something about whatever it is we're avoiding. During my years of helping families and seniors at the community level, the hardest cases where those where the communication never began, or began and never continued. Either way, assumptions prevail, choices are made (or not), things unravel, and time marches on. Inevitably, there will come a crisis point, and it will all be addressed whether the planning is done or not. You're smart to get the conversation and planning started.

There are a few guideposts to keep in mind as you organize your thoughts. You may have a plan in mind (let's say for your mother and father) that you would love to see prevail, but remember: this is their life, their chapter, and they may have a plan of their own in mind that you have no idea exists. Ask questions about their plans for the future, and see if they have an idea of what they want to see happen. (Remember Helen's nine-hundred-pound gorilla in the room, the Michigan cottage, and the sorry result of likely ignoring its presence?) If they do have a plan—even if it's vague, improbable, or overly optimistic (to you) based on health, finances, geography, or any number of other stumbling blocks—at least it's a starting place for discussion. Hear them out. Treat it seriously, honor it, even write it down, and begin thinking in terms of tweaking it, all the while being thankful that you don't have to start at the beginning and lead the discussion from ground zero.

On the other hand, if you know for certain that nothing has been done, no plans exist, and talks have never occurred about future needs (or how needs inevitably change over time, or how they plan to answer the call for change), then you have your marching orders. There are many creative ways to begin talking about future plans, but the important thing is to begin. Also, know that it's natural to feel uncomfortable about leading our elders, maybe even your mom or dad, into a topic they're reluctant to discuss. They're as uncomfortable as we are, probably even more so. Few people like to talk about their declining health or abilities (physical and/or mental), and they often perceive it as a failure on their part to be unable to do tasks they once did easily when they were younger. Even when you're careful in your tone and word selection to not sound judgmental, they still feel judged and defensive, most likely because they're judging themselves. Their decline makes them unhappy. They don't want to be at this point in their lives, feeling and seeing themselves slip into a lackluster version of who they once were.

We all carry around a mental picture of who we are, and it can be jolting to suddenly see we're no longer that person. Try to tread delicately and be compassionate. Reassure them that you're there to help only, not to take over their lives and create a new one for them that doesn't fit who they are. At the same time, though, you're a realist. You need to talk about changes in what they can and can't do for themselves, and help them map a way to make life as easy and as enjoyable as it can possibly be. They're the designer; you're the facilitator. And remember to ask questions before you tell them the way you think it should be. In fact, when you feel them withdrawing from the talk and clamming up, first ask yourself if you've been telling more than asking. More questions, less informing. If it still seems to be at an impasse, you can always say a version of, "Let's think about this and come back to it later. I'd really like to know your thoughts."

As you plan for this discussion and begin to move through it, you will find that the mental acuity of your loved one greatly influences your approach, execution, and degree of success. The first attempt at this conversation may garner nothing more for you than an understanding that you cannot continue to seek agreement as planned. If they are dealing with one of the many forms of dementia, especially diagnosed Alzheimer's, then you'll be grateful you're beginning talks as early as possible. Dementia is progressive, and conversations—especially complicated ones like this topic—become more difficult as time passes and abilities decline; the troublesome short-term memory makes it nearly impossible to finish a topic, let alone handle multiple small topics simultaneously. The more advanced the disease process, the more directive you will ultimately need to be planning and helping them, but you'll still want to strive for walking the line between taking over with your plan as the ultimate solution and listening for their wishes, hopes, and plans. It's still not about you and what you want to plan for them, unless or until they become a danger to themselves or to others. Then speed is of the essence, but you absolutely need the authority and appropriate powers to make the decisions.

There are several areas for discussion that are uncomfortable to varying degrees but necessary to explore (these broadly include finances, legal paperwork, medical issues, future plans to accommodate the effects of ageing, each being addressed individually in later chapters). One of the most important and more difficult discussions is regarding your loved one's financial picture. Money drives many of the decisions that will be made and either limits or opens up the number of choices available. As a whole, the generation we're trying to help prefers to keep their financial information close to their vests. They're very private and tend to believe their business is nobody else's business. Be prepared for this characteristic, and try not to be offended by their unwillingness to talk about their finances. Though it may feel like a trust issue, my experience is it's not personal; it's just the way this generation tends to be. Many of them were children of the Great Depression and grew up with little in terms of money or comfort. As they grew older and accumulated more of both, they were careful and protective of their gains. Now that they're older and only have limited income, they're fearful of losing control over what they struggled to build. Try to help them see that you need the full financial picture in order to help them make successful choices for the long term—that is, you don't want them to lose money with risky decisions, and you're not selfishly interested in any personal gain. They're still in control, but you'll only be as helpful to them as you are informed.

You'll also need to know what legal preparation has been put in place, if any, as protection against lost abilities and capacities as life changes from the known to the unknown. Who is going to make the decisions when they no longer can? Who will execute the countless bits of paperwork on their behalf? What are their plans, their wishes? There are a limited number of legal documents needed (each discussed in chapter 9) to successfully deal with end of life decision-making and empowerment, but they are all absolutely necessary. I have seen more cases than I care to remember of incomplete legal paperwork or, even worse, no paperwork at all, and it's always discovered mid-crisis and at the most inopportune time. Be sure your legal documents are airtight, capture your loved one's wishes completely, and place responsibility in the hands of someone who can and will execute the powers accordingly. Seriously consider spending the extra money to have an elder law attorney make sure everything is done properly. If money is an issue, there is legal assistance through county or state resources, but please don't try to do everything on your own. The Internet is a wonderful thing, but it can also make us feel more knowledgeable and capable than we actually are.

Your loved one's medical history is another area of opportunity that needs to be addressed. From my experience, this topic seems to become a point of focus in one of two unfortunate situations that I've heard retold numerous times. In one case, you've been listening to your mother's retelling of her doctor appointments, asking her great questions for more information, and you feel like you have a solid understanding of her health issues; then, for example, during an unscheduled hospitalization, you learn she has several larger chronic issues you knew nothing about. In the other case, you know your mom is seeing several specialists in addition to her general practitioner, but you're stunned when she's hospitalized from a fall that the doctor says was likely due to an overdose of prescription drugs. As frightening and maddening as these two examples are when they happen to you and someone you love, they are also fairly commonplace. Fortunately, however, changes in communication practices can go a long way toward minimizing the risk of both situations, but you need the authority (see chapters 9 and 10) and knowledge about the range of options to make them happen.

As you move through your talk, ideas about changes to their "home" and more potential care will likely keep floating into the discussion (generally unrelated to the topic you think you're discussing), but you can stay calm and focused. There are really only two over-arching choices they can make, and you can confidently go either way and handle it successfully. The parameters are limited to one of two directions: they will either want to age in place at home for as long as it is safely possible, or they will be open to senior community living and will entertain moving (see chapter 11). While you may personally prefer one over the other, you will have more than enough ammunition to make whichever direction they choose completely doable. There are plusses and minuses, positives and negatives to either choice, but there are also multiple means of bolstering your success in either direction.

At the end of gathering these large chunks of information, your goal is to put a plan in place for the benefit of your loved ones. Every family and every situation is different, and pulling together factual bits and pieces of a long life can range from remarkably easy to stunningly complicated. If your talk goes off task, if it becomes a road that seems non-linear and you find yourself trudging through detours you didn't know existed but seem to be infinitely fascinating to the storyteller, try to breathe deeply. Those detours mean something to someone whose life matters to us. Slow down and enjoy. We tend to move through this information-gathering process like we're organizing work space for the deal of the century, when what we're really doing is helping edit the last chapter of a really good, sweet book. Unless you are in the middle of a healthcare crisis and timing is of the essence, take time to hear, process, and treasure the meandering that can be a part of information gathering. You may learn things you never knew or be reminded of memories that you will treasure in years to come.

When you have enough information to determine how much thinking and planning has been completed for the future and what remains to be done, your next step is to prioritize and delegate. My hope for you is that your loved one has at least started planning, but however much remains to be completed, do your best to share the workload.

You have four distinct topics that could ideally become delegated work for several people:

1) an accurate financial picture

2) completed legal paperwork

3) a clear understanding of health issues

4) a preference to either age in place at home or to pursue senior community living

Hopefully the detail gathering can be delegated to family members or trusted confidants. Be prepared, however, that the entire process is emotional and ripe for family dysfunction, often full of openings when individual personalities show through from less than flattering vantage points. There were countless times family members shared their stories with me of how difficult the process was for them, but this is not the platform to replay old memories and hurt feelings. You're looking for commitment and cooperation to execute the plan for someone you love that needs your help, not providing a chance to air dirty family laundry. So, try to ignore the "journey" and focus on the "destination"—the end goal.

You will find that even though you research and organize your findings in terms of financial, legal, medical, and housing, the topics intertwine and mix together during discussions. For instance, it's hard to talk seriously about a living situation and needed care without a clear picture of the financial situation, but that's the approach most seniors will take for two reasons. They have no idea what senior community living or at-home care costs, and they neither know nor want to discuss how much money they think they have. They also generally know they need to have a will but are pretty vague on the rest of what is needed and why. Unless there's been a lawyer the family has routinely used in the past, the prospect of finding a good lawyer they'll like for all this "stuff" is something that can be easily put off for years; however, if you're in the leadership position and do the organizing of appointments and paperwork with and for them, relief and gratitude should (eventually) reign.

Naturally, there are delightful exceptions to these broad generalizations, and you may have your talk with someone like Beverly, one of my all-time favorite residents who, at ninety-six, is still feistily pursuing the joy in every day (which means the truth in all situations and the relationships she finds to be honest). She came to me many years ago on her own accord for an apartment in our community. Beverly was a bookkeeper her entire life, never married, and commuted daily by train some distance to her job in Chicago until she retired in her early eighties. She was fine living without a captive community of folks her own age (her perception of community living for seniors), but she had grown tired of walking for groceries and cooking for herself. Needless to say, Beverly had all of her ducks in a row, everything down to the penny, and she was ready to share copies of all possibly relevant legal documents. I'm guessing you don't have a Beverly in your life because they're few and far between, but that's okay. It only puts you in the same group with the rest of us, the vast majority of caregivers hoping and trying to do the best we can to be truly helpful facilitating a positive result.

For More Information

Erin Garrett, "Quiz: Is it time to talk to Mom and Dad about alternative senior living?" Ascend's Golden Guide, October 2013

http://www.ascendsgoldenguide.com/living-options/
quiz-when-to-talk-to-parents-about-alternative-senior-living

"Let's Talk: A Constructive Conversation," Genworth, October 2013

https://www.genworth.com/lets-talk/ltc/talking-to-loved-ones.html

"Independent Living: Starting a Dialogue," AARP, October 2010

https://member.aarp.org/relationships/caregiving-resource-center/info-10-2010/
gs_independent_living_starting_a_dialogue.html.

"Don't Wait for the Crisis," Senior Care Central

http://senior-care-central.com/alzheimers-dementia.

Naomi Freundlich, "Long-Term Care: What Are the Issues?" Robert Wood Johnson Foundation, February 2014

www.rwjf.org.

Michelle Singletary, "Don't give up trying to persuade an aging parent to move to better care," Washington Post, June 21, 2014

http://www.washingtonpost.com/pb/michelle-singletary

Michelle Singletary, "Why seniors, adult children should discuss long-term care," Washington Post, posted Sunday, June 29, 2014

http://www.roanoke.com/business/columns_and_blogs/columns/color_of_money/why-seniors-adult-children-should-discuss-long-term-care/article_f44df9de-fe24-11e3-9179-0017a43b2370.html.

Tim Prosch, The Other Talk: A Guide to Talking With Your Adult Children About the Rest of Your Life, AARP, 2014

https://member.aarp.org/entertainment/books/bookstore/home-family-caregiving/the-other-talk/

CHAPTER EIGHT

Financial Status

When you begin to construct your loved one's complete financial picture, you generally know you want to put your hands on anything that looks remotely relevant. This will include (but is not limited to) bank accounts, safe deposit boxes, vehicles, recent tax returns, income of all types (pensions, Social Security, IRAs), investments (stocks, bonds, money market funds, real estate transactions), and insurance. Alongside these items, you're also looking for debt or regular payments that function in the "debit" column. Note that some of the items—e.g., real estate and insurance—could be both an asset/credit and, with monthly payments, also a debit. It's much the same exercise as constructing a household budget, but, at least initially, for an entirely different purpose. You're not going to put them on a monthly budget, but you are going to get a feel for which desired changes are possible in both the short and long term.

My dad surprised me during an early visit to their newly purchased retirement house in North Carolina, where I was pleased to find he had organized a drawer in his desk with all relevant financial information in carefully labeled hanging files. "Come see what I've done," he beamed with the twinkling eyes of a kid who pulled off a great surprise gift, which indeed it was. In fact, it was out of character for him to be so tidy with bills, tax information, and all manner of financial papers. He had always known where everything was—somewhere on top of the dining room hutch in a mess of papers that grew in depth and width as the tax season approached, but this was something new. Even Mom beamed with pride. We marveled, praised, and performed a cursory overview of what was where, just in case that vague, far-away day eventually arrived when he would be in need of my help as Power of Attorney for finance.

That day arrived many years later but sooner than any of us expected. You're never ready for the change. By time, Mom and Dad had moved from the previously mentioned house to a two-bedroom apartment a few miles away, an "independent living" situation that eventually became unsuitable for their needs after Dad fell on the property and sustained serious injuries. I traveled to the apartment for a good visit and to organize their spare bedroom, which was to be the office-guest room but had not been unpacked or arranged. In all fairness, I had been warned that it was a mess of boxes piled on boxes, untouched and ready for sorting, all of which I could keep and file or discard at my discretion. Not a problem, I assured them.

Have you ever seen the inside of a warehouse storage unit that was packed to the gills? That's what greeted me when I opened the door to the second bedroom, and my heart sank. Although it was a huge effort just to reach the top boxes of each stack and move them down to the floor where search and rescue was possible, I very slowly made progress with the contents and tried hard not to notice how the mess was becoming far worse before it was getting better. What on earth was all of this and why was it here?

Dad was the youngest and only surviving of four sons and, through a combination of his personal inclinations and life's natural pruning of family trees, he was positioned as the keeper of his family history. I believe he felt responsible for the safekeeping of who we are and who our family had been, as represented by countless pieces of paper that easily dated back to the late-1800s. Much of the history had been inherited over the years as family members passed away, but he and Mom had done a thorough job of adding at least half of the "keepsakes."

The oldest pieces were family portraits, groupings of mostly unidentifiable people to either Mom or Dad without a name or year written on the back. We loved finding pictures of the large family gatherings at long tables covered in white tablecloths, set with silver, china, and flowers, hardwood dining room chairs carefully placed around the edges, all situated in the grassy yards of plain but large homes under sprawling shade trees. Their clothes were fascinating: women with long, sweeping skirts that brushed the ground, high necklines, and tiny, pinched waists; men in long-sleeved, high-collared white shirts, ties, and suit jackets. It appeared to be summer, but they were dressed in Sunday best that had to be stiflingly hot.

I also found things of lesser interest: boxes and boxes of canceled checks and bank statements (all Mom and Dad's going back to the late-1940s); many years of tax returns, including one from the year I was born (1952); hundreds of letters and postcards from friends and family; pictures of our immediate family (Mom and Dad's dating years and wedding through current day, plus the three of us kids from our birth through current day with our kids). Alas, there were no filed tax returns for Mom and Dad during the last several years. And, needless to say, after I could get around the boxes and locate the desk, the once greatly praised and well-organized drawer of financial papers looked much the same as it had when last viewed in the den of their house years ago. The carefully labeled files had been only minimally updated during the following years. This scene ended days later with me dragging huge bags of trash through the living room onto the balcony, and then rolling them over the railing to drop on the grass below near the rented dumpster. The room came together as envisioned, mostly, and their taxman was on the case with some long days ahead.

I offer you my personal illustration as a friendly warning: you simply don't know what kind of situation you'll encounter when you go looking for your loved one's financial picture. Time passes and situations change, but you may not want to be lured into thinking that they've got it covered just because you've been shown an organized drawer of financial files. My dad was many things, including being a perfectionist and a lover of disparate elements coming together with precision . . . just not about anything related to paying bills. My advice is to get on the hunt now and, as much as possible, stay on it as life changes. In reality, if they need your help now, then they're only going to need it more as time passes. You'll ultimately be glad later for every hour you spend pulling things together now.

When you have arrived at what you feel is a clear understanding of their finances, there are a few caveats I'd like to address. First, be certain that when you go through the math to arrive at how many months or years of assets exist against anticipated monthly costs, you have to remember to add in monthly income. This may sound overly simplistic, but I've witnessed the confusion too often. For example, Suzie—and a good number of other panicked individuals—told me that her mother, age eighty-five, was able to finance only three years of private pay (say, assets of $150,000 against $4000/month projected rent and care) before they had to find government assistance for her housing and care needs. In reality, Suzie, et.al, had forgotten that Mom gets $3,000/month in assorted income, thereby drawing down only $1,000/month from her $150,000, which will last her for 12.5 years. Don't panic.

Second, take the time to ask questions of your loved one about their investment strategies and, more particularly, what they were hoping to achieve when they purchased parts of their portfolio. A close friend of mine, who I consider to be an accounting and finance guru, wished she had taken this opportunity with her father before he passed away. The issues that came up with his estate were not questions for an elder law attorney or even a financial planner; instead, they were triggers for conversations she wished had taken place regarding choices he made, plans he had, and his hopes for the future. The point is, the time to ask questions, learn, and connect the dots will soon be gone, so have the conversations now. Have the talks and get the information while you can.

Third, after you have the financial picture in mind and are considering options for how to pay for the choices of your loved one, there are exclusions that will not help you when you thought they might. One of the rudest awakenings of my life occurred at the first senior community I investigated for Mom and Dad long before they moved near me from North Carolina, and I checked out the information I'd been given at following locations simply because I couldn't believe I'd been told the truth. Medicare, into which they had paid all of their working careers, and any other health insurance, will not pay one penny toward "custodial care," the technical term for assisted living. I had a hard time believing that the accrued expense and benefits of those insurances did not reach the cost of care for seniors when they needed help with the activities of daily living they could no longer perform by themselves . . . but it's absolutely true. Even with a doctor's verification? No, not even with a doctor's sworn and signed affidavit, plus the promise of his firstborn thrown in to boot.

You'll be grateful many times over for Medicare and supplemental insurance during hospitalizations, rehabilitation, nursing home stays, doctors' office visits, and possibly for pharmaceutical expenses, but it will never touch the ongoing costs of rent and care at a senior community.

Lastly, some good news: there are a limited number of ways to possibly get financial help that you should investigate. If they are applicable, you'll breathe a sigh of relief. First, be certain whether or not your loved one secured a Long-Term Care insurance policy, which is designed specifically to cover care charges or, more specifically, the assistance or nursing care costs in assisted living and nursing homes. You'll also want to see parallel language in the policy covering the same cost of care at home verses a community living setting. As I've mentioned before, only somewhere between 8 percent and 12 percent of seniors have long-term care policies in effect, but it is a beautiful thing when you find it and it functions to the senior's benefit. Be warned, however: the devil is in the details.

There are many versions of long-term care policies floating around, all of them somewhere on the continuum between god-sent and worthless for what you may want. I will never forget this adorable, tiny lady in her late eighties who fell in love with her vision of what life could be like for her on our assisted-living floor. She had been paying for her long-term care policy for more than twenty years, and she was so thrilled that she could afford this newly envisioned life with us. Unfortunately, more than twenty years ago, assisted living was barely a sparkle in someone's eyes. Her policy was written for nursing homes only, and though some companies will cover a change to the newer concept, hers would not. This sweet lady was much too healthy and spry for a nursing home, but her options were limited. Check out the fine print, call with questions, and get answers in writing. You'll be glad you spent the time on this one.

Another possibility is the Veteran's Aide and Attendance benefit administered through the Department of Veteran's Affairs (VA). This applies to veterans (and un-remarried surviving spouses) who served during wartime years (combat isn't necessary), are over age sixty-five, and who need help paying for care. The threshold requirement is at least ninety days of active service, one day of which is active service during the specific dates of war:

WWII: 12/7/1941 through 12/31/1946

Korean Conflict: 6/27/1950 through1/31/1955

Vietnam War: 8/5/1964 through 5/7/1975, although veterans who served in Vietnam itself ("in country") as early as 2/28/1961 may also qualify

Dates of service can be verified from discharge papers, which must show an honorable discharge.

How much potential money is involved in monthly benefits through this program? It's enough to make the difference between being able to afford community living and not. The surviving spousal benefit (the individual was married to a veteran who fit the program's criteria, the veteran is no longer living, and the spouse did not remarry a non-veteran) is $1,130 per month. A veteran himself or herself can receive up to $1,758 per month, and a veteran living with a spouse (a veteran and non-veteran couple) may receive $2,085. If a married couple consists of two qualified veterans, the amount is even higher. There's also a pension if a veteran, who is still independent but who is caring for a sick spouse whose medical expenses completely deplete their combined monthly income: the veteran may be eligible to file as a Veteran with a Sick Spouse and to receive $1,380 per month.

Once you get past the initial hurdle of dates and other qualifying criteria, there are many other rules, regulations, and precise definitions that must be combed through carefully. My advice is to not skip over even one of them, especially the ones that seem the stickiest and most difficult to understand. I've learned over the years that like all government agencies, the VA has no sense of humor where Aid and Attendance is concerned.

For instance, one of the rules that's fairly straight-forward is that the veteran can no longer be driving a car. An often retold anecdotal tale of how serious the VA is about their rules being maintained involves some clever seniors somewhere in southern Illinois who thought the no-driving rule was ridiculous. So, they kept on driving after they started receiving the benefit. The VA found out about one individual who was still driving against regulation and decided to check all of the veterans receiving the benefit at that particular senior-living community. They found a large group of payees in violation and still driving, billed them back for the entire amount of Aid and Attendance benefits paid to them over the years, and cut off any further future payments. This caused all of them to leave the community they could no longer afford, and the community itself was allegedly pending bankruptcy. So the story goes, and whether it's completely true or not, it illustrates well what could happen.

The application process is not an easy one, even with the best and most ethical professional helping to get matters lined up for the application's submission to the VA. You can count on an average of nine months following the submission of the application to the VA before a conclusion is reached and (hopefully) monthly benefits begin reaching your loved one. You also need to understand that there is no "sure thing" in regards to results. I've seen VA decisions appealed time and time again, and the wait is no faster the second or third time around. You need to get it right the first time, and that means on every little detail. There have been more than a few times that the veteran passed away before the final decision could be made, and there's no accommodation for money due to the estate.

Also, the senior must be living in an assisted-living community and receiving the daily help that's needed when the application is submitted to the VA and while pending approval; therefore, during this time, the senior must pay privately for rent and care. There is actually a section on the application that must be completed by the community itself where the veteran is residing. Depending on the community, you may be able to negotiate a reduced rate during the waiting period, the accrued balance due in full when the benefit comes through. Quite frankly, though, the vast majority of communities that once were glad to help in this way no longer do. The risk is just too high for the amount of time and money involved, and they've been burned quite a few times. Nevertheless, it's worth a try and never hurts to ask.

Many communities will have a professional with whom they have worked and who will help the community's veterans progress toward obtaining the Veterans Aid and Attendance benefit. They may invite you to a seminar at the community to be given by this individual. By all means, go to the seminar and gather information. But feel free not to commit to being shepherded by that individual through the application process until you find out how many people in the community his/her organization has successfully helped obtain the full benefit. You can also ask to talk with a few of the residents who are getting the benefit about how helpful (or not) the individual was: overall, how they felt about the application process with the guidance provided?

There are many professionals who make a living helping senior veterans and their families wade through the application's finer points, but you need to feel comfortable you can enjoy a high level of trust with this individual. I personally appreciate it when there's the oversight of an elder law attorney involved in the process. Many companies offering to help seniors have an elder law attorney in their structure, but most one- or two-person offices operate without this oversight. If you're on the fence about deciding to work with any individual, then ask for referrals.

Every year the Veteran's Administration gets Congressional approval for funding this program, so the money is there, waiting. But as I used to tell my potential community residents, the government will never come knocking on your door with the information it has money waiting for you. You have to do the dirty work. I've only given you the broadest of details on the program for the simple reason that the Aid and Attendance benefit could be a book in itself. I've helped many people get started on the process and made information available to them so they believe it's the real deal (even though they often had never heard of the program). It may initially sound as though it's too good to be true, but I've rejoiced with residents and family members alike when the letter of acceptance arrived and the first check quickly followed.

There are other VA pension programs for seniors who are home-bound and choosing to remain at home, but the Aid and Attendance program is for those choosing senior community living to fulfill their health concerns and needs. In this case, when the final application is submitted to the VA and the senior veteran is residing in the community setting at that time—i.e., it cannot be a prospective plan of action; you have to be

IN the community—then the initial check is a retroactive payment back to the date of application AND the monthly payments also begin. Again, I've seen unhappy family members who did not receive the full amount retroactively that they had anticipated, so find the fine print and make sure you have followed precisely what needs to be done.

Finally, a Reverse Mortgage is another option to help fund choices for your senior. You've probably seen many advertisements for reverse mortgages, both on television and as the subject of direct mailings. To me, the advertising is almost always overly optimistic and borders on being very misleading, but in certain limited circumstances you may find a reverse mortgage helpful and something you want to investigate. At the very least, it shouldn't be surprising if your loved one is familiar with the term, whether or not it applies to their situation.

A Reverse Mortgage, also known as a Home Equity Conversion Mortgage (HECM), allows the mortgagee (age sixty-two or older) to tap into the equity that has built up in their home over the years and use it to supplement their income. The senior must own the home free and clear, or the mortgage balance has to be cleared with the proceeds from the loan at closing. Here is the trick: the proceeds can be spent in any way desired, as long as the "spenders" are living in the home to which the loan is tied. In other words, as HUD (department of Housing and Urban Development) puts it, "Use Your Home to Stay at Home." You cannot use the proceeds from a reverse mortgage to finance living at a senior community, but you can use it to make modifications and get nursing assistance to age in place at home.

I dealt with a senior couple's daughter during two very long phone conversations during work one day. She insisted her parents could easily afford community living expenses—despite low monthly Social Security payments, no pension payments, and minimal savings—because they had just received a lump sum payment from their recently approved reverse mortgage. When I explained that to enjoy the proceeds, her parents had to remain living in the home that served as the basis of the loan, she was incredulous and, quite frankly, thought I was nuts.

"But you must be wrong," she said, "because they were told they could use the money however they want."

"Yes," I said, "as long as they live in the house."

The theme of the second call was that if I were correct (which she still doubted) that her parents' choices were so severely limited, how would anyone ever know the difference if they instead used the money to finance an apartment at a senior community? Needless to say, her parents were not a "move in" at my community.

Lenders backed by the Federal Housing Authority (FHA) have ways and means to insure all goes as intended, t's are crossed and i's are dotted. I offer reverse mortgages only as another option, which you may or may not find useful if your loved ones want to remain at home and age in place. If you decide to pursue more information, please search for people you like and trust and who have all of the appropriate accreditation. Understand that as reverse mortgages have increased in popularity, so have the number of less than reputable offerings.

For More Information

"Federal Benefits for Veterans, Dependents, and Survivors," Office of Public and Governmental Affairs, accessed June 15, 2014

va.gov/opa/publications/benefits_book.asp

"The Aid & Attendance Improved Pension," accessed June 19, 2014

http://www.veteranaid.org/ptogram.php

http://www.veteranaid.org/docs/21-534.pdf (surviving spouse)

http://www.veteranaid.org/docs/21-526.pdf (veteran)

"Fact Sheets, Veterans Benefits Administration," U.S. Department of Veterans Affairs, accessed June 15, 2014

http://www.benefits.va.gov/BENEFITS/factsheets.asp

http://www.archives.gov/veterans/military-service-records

(request lost discharge papers)

"Guide to Veteran's Benefit," A Place for Mom, accessed June 15, 2014

http://aplaceformom.com/senior-care-resources/articles/
benefits-for-veterans-and-their-spouses.

"Guide to Financing Senior Care," A Place for Mom, accessed June 15, 2014

http://www.aplaceformom.com/financial-assistance.

Patty Servaes (Elder Resource Benefits Consulting), "The VA Pension Benefit – Don't Take No for an Answer," Senior Living Smart, June 2014

http://www.seniorlivingsmart.com/best-kept-secrets-va-benefit.

Home Equity Conversion Mortgages for Seniors, HUD FHA Reverse Mortgage for Seniors (HECM), accessed June 23, 2014

http://portal.hud.gov/hudportal/HUD?src=/program_offices/housing/sfh/hecmhome.

CHAPTER NINE

Legal Preparation

We used to go to lawyers to handle anything even remotely sounding legal or having the possibility of growing into something legal. Now, computers and the Internet have made it easy to access forms and instructions for completing all sorts of legal documents that were traditionally handled for us by attorneys. You can complete certain legal documents without a lawyer, and doing so as a rough draft or as an exercise to order your thoughts might actually be a very good idea. It never hurts to do pre-planning against a template of what's required by law.

When you're in the process of making certain your loved one's legal paperwork accurately captures their wishes, however, it can be especially helpful to get advice and services from a board-certified elder law attorney. Similar to shopping for a physician specialist, board certification tells you that the lawyer has specialized knowledge, skills, and proficiency in a specific area of law—in this case, elder law—and their expertise is grounded in the highest possible level of professionalism and ethical decision-making in the practice of law. They are the experts. Whether you seek guidance for long-range estate planning or you simply have a few questions about documents needed for your loved one's peace of mind, an appointment with an Elder Law attorney will bring order to chaos.

There are several documents that you need to be certain your loved one has finalized—completed, signed properly, and filed where you know they can be grabbed at a moment's notice. There are four key documents:

Living Will

Power of Attorney for Healthcare

Power of Attorney for Finance

Last Will and Testament.

Beyond these necessities there are many topics—for instance, guardianship, conservatorship, and issues regarding competency; Medicare, Medicaid, or Social Security questions; elder exploitation, abuse, or neglect—that may need to be addressed sometime later, but now is the time to be certain these four key documents have been handled.

If any of these documents have already been executed, it's probably the Last Will and Testament. Most people know what a Will is, and they probably think they need to make one. If your loved one has a small estate and doesn't think it's necessary to make a Will, encourage them to think again. A Will ensures their money and property will be distributed according to their wishes: it gives them power and control. Your loved one worked hard to accumulate whatever they have, and a Will lets them control who gets what. Without a Will, the state divvies up all assets according to local laws, and your loved one will get no say whatsoever regarding the disbursement of assets from their life's work. Since a Will has no effect until after your loved one has passed away, however, the other three documents are of more immediate interest to what you're trying to accomplish.

Together, a Living Will and Healthcare Power of Attorney (also known as Healthcare Surrogate or Healthcare Proxy) are often called Advance Directives, which serve to record medical preferences. There are state law variations in the name of the documents, the title of the named individual within, and even the number of witnesses to the signing. You and your loved one don't have to work with an attorney to create Advance Directives, but state law might require signing documents in the presence of one or more witness. If you have even a brief appointment with an Elder Law attorney, any questions will be immediately resolved and you'll know once and for all that everything is correct. This will provide peace of mind, not only for your loved one but also for you as well.

Living Will: This document directs decision-making regarding life-sustaining treatment in a terminal situation (illness or injury) when your loved one can no longer make or express their own wishes. At some future time, if they lose their ability to make decisions or express their wishes, the Living Will records end-of-life medical choices previously made by them when they had the ability to do so. It clarifies for both family members and medical professionals how this individual directs their own end-of-life medical treatments: do they accept or decline life-sustaining measures? They first decide what type of treatment they want (or do not want); then secondly, they select the person to whom they give authority to act for them (as they would for themselves, if they could) when they no longer have the ability to express themselves. Substituted decision-making is created so their wishes are executed accordingly if the time arrives and it's necessary.

The decision to accept or decline life-sustaining treatment is a deeply personal one, shaped through a lifetime by an individual's beliefs, values, and experiences. You may find yourself needing to encourage your loved one's thinking on this point: there is no right or wrong answer, only what they wish for themselves. In selecting an individual to act for them in a substituted capacity, they need to choose someone who can and will ensure their decisions are properly executed—free of influence from family members or friends who might have different opinions. Perhaps the best way to accomplish this is through open communication with family and physicians. Tell them about decisions and expectations before the emotions of trauma or failing health take hold of the situation.

Aging with Dignity, an online resource (www.agingwithdignity. org), offers a template to record medical treatment preferences. Called "Five Wishes," the completed document meets legal requirements of an Advance Directive in forty-two states. In all states (and particularly in the remaining states where "Five Wishes" cannot stand alone as an Advance Directive), it is often attached to the state's legal form as an addendum offering more information. The popularity of "Five Wishes" perhaps lies in how personal and individualized the requests can become when one looks beyond purely medical treatment. For example, they might find comfort in soft music playing continually in the background, favorite poems or books being read out loud, or knowing that the request for prayers will be passed along and honored. They could find aromatherapy or gentle message with scented lotions to be soothing. Perhaps they would enjoy vases of freshly cut flowers. Whatever wishes one has for their comfort, peace, and quiet pleasure when they're unable to explain their own desires, "Five Wishes" provides a means of communicating how help can be provided.

Healthcare Power of Attorney (POA/HC): A power of attorney is a written document in which the "principal" (for example, your mother) appoints someone else (an "agent" or "attorney in fact") to act on her behalf in limited circumstances. The document creates substituted decision-making: the agent acts in place of the principal, for the principal, as the principal would act for herself if she could. The appointed individual (and an alternate agent in case the primary agent is unavailable) advocates for the patient on a range of medical treatments set out in the document, not just the life-prolonging measures discussed in Living Wills. The patient, your loved one, makes decisions recorded in the document about various treatment options; the healthcare agent makes decisions only when the patient can't communicate on her own. Many states combine this document with a Living Will into one form, while others maintain separate forms.

It's my opinion that the POA/HC's usage rate—the sheer number of times it must be produced to enable communication with, for example, a treating physician—makes it the number-one item on your "to-do" list. Prior to passage of HIPAA (Health Insurance Portability & Accountability Act) and its regulations in 1996, communication in hospitals with treating physicians and their staff was a lot less complicated than it is now. Since privacy laws have been tightened by both HIPAA regulations and by practitioners' interpretation of them, you must be able to produce a copy of your POA for Healthcare designation whenever your identity is in question; otherwise, you will not be included in discussions about your loved one's medical treatment. Absurdity can ensue, as was the case with one of my mom's hospitalizations. Granted, reliance on computerization has at least quickened the speed with which communications travel, but the principles remain the same.

My mother's second broken hip, which happened in the middle of the night during a trip to the bathroom in her apartment, is a good example of what can go wrong with paperwork—and often does. Mom, in her early nineties at the time, was residing in a senior living community where I worked as director of marketing. In the middle of the night,

I received a call from our security department—never a good thing—that the resident below Mom's apartment had heard a loud "thud" in the apartment above, followed by pounding noises on her ceiling, and she wondered if security could check it out and make sure everything's okay.

Luckily for Mom, the resident below had excellent hearing. The noise occurred when Mom fell in her bathroom, deeply gouging her head on the corner of a table midway down to the ceramic tile floor, landing hard enough to break her hip. The intermittent noise on the resident's ceiling was Mom pounding the bathroom floor with her fist, trying to get someone's attention (she couldn't move to the emergency pull cord and forgot she was wearing a medic alert bracelet). Security quickly called paramedics, who were speeding Mom and her paperwork to the hospital emergency room down the street, and then called me. By the time I got to the hospital, she had been prepped and was in surgery for her broken hip.

It took me awhile to put together what the communication problem really was. I saw Mom as soon as she was out of recovery and in her hospital room, still very groggy, but receiving a flurry of bedside care. However, I had questions, and nobody seemed to have the answers. The surgeon had left the hospital immediately following Mom's operation and was starting a planned vacation out of state. His operating notes were in route, but after a shift change, no one knew anything about Mom's operation. Much later, someone said there was no paperwork at the hospital showing I was Mom's POA: no one could or would talk to me about her health and treatment without proof of who I was. Looking back, I suppose I was allowed into Mom's room as a hospital visitor, not as her POA for Healthcare, because I certainly couldn't receive information or make decisions on her behalf. I may as well have been part of the wallpaper. Naturally by the time this all came to light, the hospital record department was closed for the day.

After retracing what happened in her apartment bathroom, the call to the paramedics, and her trip to the hospital, I'm certain her medical information and Advance Directives were sent with her in the ambulance. (I know this because the front desk failed to keep a copy for our own records; they sent the only one.) What happened to the papers once she arrived at the emergency room, I have no idea. I'm also convinced that all hospital personnel truly believed they had not seen the POA paperwork, though they had dissected information pertinent to their own departments from the packet that arrived with her in the ambulance.

So I scrambled for another copy of her POA/Healthcare document from my records at home, worked around the hospital record department's hours, meal breaks, and meetings—and then waited for the "proof" to circulate to people within the hospital. I felt relief: they would believe I was who I said I was! But here's what happened in the meantime—to her, to me, and quite possibly to you (if you don't carry copies of this document with you in your car, which I learned too late).

The worst incident will give you an idea of what was happening without my knowledge. The night after her hip surgery, Mom climbed out of her bed and fell, beside her bed, on the hip with a new socket and pin. I've learned that older people, especially ones with cardiac issues, take an especially long time to clear anesthesia from their bodies, so at over ninety years old with congestive heart failure, she certainly wasn't clear-headed at the moment of escape from her bed. But to her credit, sort of, she was investigating her suspicions of a "burglar in her apartment" . . . not clear-headed enough to realize she was in a hospital room and it was the night attendant, not a burglar, cleaning her bathroom. Fortunately, tests (conducted in the middle of the night) revealed no additional damage was done to her hip.

Unbeknownst to me that anything had happened during the night, I arrived at the hospital the next morning to find nurses in a heated discussion about what to do with my mom— restraints of one type or another? A "sitter" to watch her around the clock? What's going on? It became an even more heated discussion when I eventually found out, and in bits and pieces from different people, what my mother had been through the night before, without my knowledge, without a call to inform me, because they didn't recognize my relationship to her. The nurses were still holding back and trying not to include me in the loud discussion because they had no proof I was Mom's POA. I immediately produced my copy of the POA for Healthcare. A copy of it would do them no good, they said, because it had to be on their form; they would have to wait for it to arrive from Records. No, they couldn't just call and have them fax a copy to them. That was when I went for a hard copy from Records to hand deliver it myself, and communication began.

The nurses assured me that Mom had been given plenty of information about her surgery. The surgeon (prior to his departure for vacation) had talked to Mom (in the Recovery Room!), and his replacement had spoken with her very early that morning (after the traumatic "burglar" episode, the fall, and several tests in the middle of the night at the opposite end of the hospital!). The nurses swore they had talked to Mom and given her explicit instructions several times about not walking on her own. They felt she was simply disobeying them. Since they had no proof I was her POA at the time she fell, they couldn't call to notify me about the nighttime "escape" from her bed and the necessary tests.

My first act was to specify absolutely no restraints; they would have to find someone to sit by her bedside and keep her from climbing out of it again. And they also began paying attention when I answered their questions, chief among them, "No, she doesn't have Alzheimer's," and "No, she's doesn't have behavioral issues." And this one, which caused problems (temporarily): "Yes, the records are correct. She resides in an independent apartment in a senior-living community. They appeared incredulous that Mom did very well in her "home" setting, implying that I wasn't involved with her life to really know (". . . well, how often do you really see her?"). From what they had observed, a nursing home was a more appropriate, safer setting. I tried very hard to politely explain (not in an attempt to be a "good girl," but because these people were giving care to my mother when I couldn't be there, and I really didn't want to alienate them) that they were seeing her in an exceptionally difficult situation, not in normal day-to-day activities. I thought to myself, these are trained nurses? Then the conversation would return to variations on behavioral questions about dementia, which she didn't have, and we'd start all over again.

Hopefully, your experience dealing with your loved one's traumatic health event will be different than this particular one I'm recalling. Hopefully, getting a copy of your POA paperwork from Point A to Point B will be more efficiently handled. This much, however, I can say for certain. If there has been an operation with the patient under anesthesia, and if that patient is, in fact, your loved one who happens to be in the later years of life, then knowing a few things in advance will ease your experience.

No matter what training has been done for nurses and aides, there is a predisposition that still exists with many of them about elderly patients: they require more work, more time, and don't remember a thing they're told. Your presence during your loved one's stay is really the only way to be assured that everyone's behavior is respectfully appropriate. Why?

The staff will always claim they were respectful. And the patient was told x, y, z, and said they understood. The patient just doesn't remember. Well . . . maybe, maybe not. If you aren't there to confirm the presence or absence of the conversation – maybe they really weren't told x, y, z. The "playing field" is not exactly level.

The anesthesia clears the patient's system slowly, and their mind during the process doesn't work the way it normally does. Short-term memory is seriously hampered. And, additionally, hallucinations can be a temporary but complicating part of the recovery—they were for Mom— which doesn't help your case in convincing others that your loved one does not have dementia, Alzheimer's, or behavioral issues.

Whether or not your loved one makes an "ideal" patient for the nurses (Lord knows, my mother likely was not at times) depends a great deal on the personality of the nurse and their skill at handling the patients—not a medical skill but a "soft" skill. If you get a good one, treat them like gold.

The best thing that you can do to avoid mishaps is to be certain the completion of Power of Attorney for Healthcare is number one on your "to-do" list. You never know when an accident can happen, changing life in a blink of the eye. Once completed, and to make sure there are no surprises, carry a few copies in a folder kept in your car. I carried copies of my original POA/Healthcare and copies of the completed home hospital's POA form as well. Let's hope mine was a unique situation where a hospital's own form trumped a legal document, but you never know. Like the Boy Scouts, our motto needs to be, Be Prepared.

Power of Attorney for Finance: This power of attorney is a written document in which the "principal" (your loved one, let's say your father) appoints someone else (possibly you, as an "agent" or "attorney in fact") to assist with finances, either now or in the future, to act with him or for him should he become unable to act for himself. Like the POA/Healthcare, this document presents the opportunity for your loved one to proactively accomplish what cannot be done if, sometime in the future, unforeseeable health events leave him incapacitated. Better to act now, select someone implicitly trusted as "agent," and give them authority to make financial decisions as the situation requires. Should he become incapacitated before a POA/Finance has been completed, the principal's family will be consumed by an expensive and lengthy process of going through the courts for appointment of a guardian or conservator to make financial decisions.

Your loved one will determine the limits of the POA/Finance, deciding exactly how much power the agent will have. The powers can range from a single transaction (the eminent selling of a specific piece of real estate, for example) to very broad, plenary powers. Anything the principal could do for himself (for example, accessing all accounts, signing all transactions, overseeing preparation and signing of tax returns, buying or selling stocks) can be done by an agent if the principal gives the power to do so. The principal and agent should both understand, however, that access for the agent to assets is not the same as joint ownership of the assets. The agent can only spend and withdraw funds for the principal's benefit.

I experienced a shocking tale involving an adorably devoted couple who moved into a community where I worked and, as often happens, the move itself was the nudge they needed to do all of the necessary legal paperwork. It's the story of a POA/Finance and the delegation of powers that went badly, a son who was appointed agent and abused the delegated powers, the relatively small bank accounts that became empty, and the son and daughter-in-law who disappeared completely. Not only were the parents financially broke and struggling to maintain their dignity, they were also heartbroken. Should you become the agent under the POA/Finance, then understand your "power" arrives hand-in-hand with fiduciary responsibility—the highest, most ethical relationship of utmost trust that is possible between two or more people. The son could have been sued for abusing the trust given to him, but I don't know how the story ended. I only know the couple had to move out of the community (where they were beloved by all) and into the daughter's home to live with her. Moral of the story: this can be a big deal, but it doesn't have to be. Just understand your job, your limits, and respect them.

It will also help to understand that the principal doesn't just "turn over the keys to the vault," so to speak, when he signs the POA/Finance and then disappear; simply disappearing and not doing for themselves what they can do is an anathema to most people. Imagine yourself . . . how would you feel if you could still write checks and balance your checkbook, but your newly appointed POA insists on doing it for you? Pretty angry, I suspect. If you're certain there is a reason to assume this responsibility--irregularities such as bills being paid more than one or not at all, checks not being recorded, significant and consistent mathematical errors--that point toward difficulty handling the task, then talk about what's going on. Ask how he feels about sharing the responsibility, or maybe having you assume some of the duties, then more as needs change. You could offer to provide a recap to him after you complete a task, keeping him abreast of your actions on his behalf. The point is, have a grace period, a time in which you can share the responsibility task rather than just taking over everything, leaving him feeling small, unimportant, and unable to handle his own affairs.

My own experience as POA/Finance for my parents was spectacularly uneventful, and I wish the same for you. It largely consisted of putting together paperwork for the accountant who did their tax returns and keeping up with their monthly bills, most of which seemed at the time to be related to medical expenses. The good part was that it was simple. The flipside of that was the reason it was simple: their assets diminished quickly with failing health, and there simply wasn't anything complicated about it. For many of you reading this book, I understand you may be dealing with larger assets and much more complicated duties. The very best advice I can give you, no matter how complicated or simple the task at hand, is to have a board-certified Elder Law attorney—one you like and trust—on speed dial, and run all questions and concerns by them, always. You'll sleep much better.

For More Information

Lawrence A. Frolik and Linda S. Whitton, Everyday Law for Seniors, Paradigm Publishers, 2012.

Paul T. Czepiga, "The 'Power' In a Power of Attorney," ElderCareMatters.com, accessed April 9, 2014

http://www.eldercarematters.com/eldercarearticles.

"Five Wishes," Aging with Dignity, accessed August 19, 1914

http://www.agingwithdignity.org/five-wishes.php.

CHAPTER TEN

Medical History

You will best be able to address your loved one's medical status and to productively support communication after you've been delegated authority as healthcare "agent" or "proxy" (Power of Attorney for Healthcare). Most likely, the clarity you're seeking regarding medical "history" will be formed in detail from that point forward, not backward. Sure, you can fill in big gaps from memory: What year was her breast cancer operation? When was prostate cancer discovered and what was the treatment? But you'll have exact dates and information from this point forward. You can still do plenty of helpful tasks prior to being made the agent for healthcare, but your attitude will be different once the delegation has been made. There's a certain sense of responsibility that cloaks your intent, and you begin to put together information in an order that's helpful to the principal/your loved one, to the doctor, to close family members, and certainly to yourself.

One of the first things you might consider doing post-POA/HC delegation is to make a list. Find your father's primary care physician, then all other physician specialists and providers (cardiology, gastroenterology, hearing, podiatry, therapy), and capture contact information for all. These are the professionals who should receive a copy of the POA/Healthcare. You can get it to them in any manner you want, from taking it on the next appointment, to mailing, emailing, faxing, or hand delivering it any day you're in the neighborhood. If you use any method besides handing it to the administrative assistant behind the desk, though, you had better call first and tell them what you're sending, what method of delivery you're using, and when to expect it. After every professional has a copy, you should be able to talk with any of them when questions arise.

The next thing you'll find helpful is to combine the physician's list with a place you can add notes. It can be on your computer, laptop, cell phone, or in a paper notebook. It doesn't really matter as long as it's easy to access, portable, and you'll use it., Begin with the day's date whenever you want to make an entry, which I was always leaving off and later trying to reconstruct, and include whatever is noteworthy. It can be a physician's summary from a call or conversation, a puzzling comment you want to later explore in some way, observation notes moving through a health event, or complaints or kudos regarding care received during hospitalization or rehabilitation services. It can be whatever you want it to be. But for your own sanity, organization, and for the simple pleasure of not having to look everywhere to find certain scraps of paper, consider making an effort to put it all in one place. We don't usually project the length of time or the number of paper scraps involved in our jobs as caretakers.

I'm sure we've all had disappointing—okay, let's admit it, alarming—conversations with our parents following an important doctor's appointment. All we get in answer to our questions is versions of "it went fine" and "he thinks I'm doing really well." Maybe that really was their (legitimate) take-away from the appointment, or maybe, just maybe they're forgetting the most salient, most difficult part, whatever that may be. Now, post-POA/HC delegation, there's no question that you can and should attend their doctor appointments if it's appropriate, if you want to, and if you can be there.

What's "appropriate" and what if you can't attend? Appropriate means there's something going on—changes in physical well-being, changes in behavior or attitude, anything that concerns you or your loved one—that needs a physician's clarification, an order for testing, or simply support for a point of view. Our parents' generation waits for the doctor's opinion before believing what we say and/or acting for themselves, and the sooner we simply accept that bit of who they are, the sooner we become free of irritation and can help accomplish what needs to be done. Learn to use their need to "hear it from the doctor" by just making the doctor's appointment, if necessary (or offering to make it), and seeing that the appointment is kept.

What if you can't attend the appointment? If you're actively using or are about to start using your status as POA for Healthcare, then I'm going to assume the senior in your life has, to some degree, declining health and is receiving some assistance with activities of daily living. If a Home Health agency is involved in their care, then I would turn to them first. Tell them about the upcoming doctor appointment and ask for one of their professionals to take your loved one, make notes, and talk with you afterward. There will be an additional charge for this, but it's worth the coordination and the price, especially if it's someone your loved one already knows. If there are friends or neighbors who can drive, who regularly visit or help out and who are willing and able to do this, then they also represent possible substitutions for you in a pinch.

Or, you can call the doctor (or physician assistant) yourself with questions after the appointment. When my parents still lived in North Carolina and my brothers and I were keeping tabs long distance, there were long stretches of time when I made many calls from Chicago to the doctors involved in Dad's hospitalizations. Sometimes that's the best you can do. Eventually I met some of them face to face, but prior to that they always returned my calls and were very open, very helpful.

You'll find the mix of options and the answers that work for you and your situation. Even though I can point out what I learned for myself with my parents and through the many relationships I built with seniors and their families, there is no one answer for everyone that is strictly The Only Way to do many of the tasks we're called upon to do as caregivers. Now that you are likely the primary caregiver and the POA/Healthcare combined, your plate is very full. Ultimately, though, you're the only one who can decide how to tackle that overflowing plate . . . call by call, appointment by appointment, and decision by decision.

CHAPTER ELEVEN

The Parameters of Home

You've been reassured that making changes to your loved one's "home" can move only in one of two directions—aging at home or embracing senior community living—and I've told you that you will be equipped to deal successfully with either choice that's made. You may feel your loved one(s) leaning in one direction or another, or you may be lucky enough to hear a preference firmly stated. Whether or not there's a preference at this stage, it may be your best opportunity to make time for a thorough comparison by talking through the positives and negatives of both options. Consider this to be discussion time rather than who-does-what to implement a solution. You have to find the direction first. The trick is going to be to make the discussion conversational, not the equivalent of a PowerPoint presentation of bulleted topics under two separate headings labeled "home" and "community."

Do you remember independent-minded Robert and his niece Leigh from chapter 3? Robert's trouble with an assisted-living community was all about the labels: he had been "independent" for ninety-five years and wasn't about to let someone else do everything for him at this stage of his life. While the difference between independent living and assisted living is a common misunderstanding for seniors exploring options, I'm afraid it's not the most likely one you may encounter when talking with your loved one about "home" choices. What you're more apt to hear as a justification for staying home and not moving is, "I will not go to a nursing home; I won't! I'm staying HOME!"

When this proclamation is made, you'll likely not even be talking about helping your mother move to a nursing home. You'll probably be describing an assisted-living community, a place where she has her own apartment full of her own furniture and belongings, restaurant-style meals, activities, entertainment, transportation options, and nursing care available (at an additional cost) for activities of daily living that have become difficult for her to perform by herself. In comparison, nursing homes operate in a more restrictive environment and require a physician's order for round-the-clock nursing care. She's thinking of a hospital-like environment: the individual can no longer remain in the hospital, but since they still need help, they go to a nursing home. The rooms are shared, as are the bathrooms; the doctors and nursing staff make routine rounds; therapy services are extensive. Nursing homes are a need, but assisted-living communities represent a choice.

The problem behind vehement reactions to nursing homes is this: somewhere, sometime in our lives, nearly all of us have had someone we love die a tragic death in a depressing, smelly nursing home, and we've proclaimed to ourselves and others that the same fate will not befall us. During the years between that event and now, nursing homes have improved, cleaned up, redecorated, increased service offerings, and sought employees who respect the concept of customer service. Nevertheless, the memory lingers, and that is often what's behind the "I'm not moving!"

This scenario is why I suggest using your current opportunity to dig deeper, ask questions, offer new information, converse, and communicate. Go beyond simply accepting a flat assertion that "I'm doing this" or "I'll never do that." See if it's well grounded in today's realities instead of long-time memories. If you handle the conversation well and it's thorough, you may reveal some misplaced, outdated "truths" getting in the way of planning for the situation at hand.

We've discussed that the vast majority of seniors say they want to age in place at home for as long as it's safely possible. Let's say that is your mother's expressed wish. Your corresponding goal is then to start a conversation that gently probes for signs of a steadfast, genuine desire to remain home with a plan that supports her success, both now and in the future. Both parts—staying at home and having a plan—need to be made with her eyes wide open. This means she not only loves her house as it has been in the past and is today, but she's also committed to necessary tweaks and changes that may be necessary as she continues to decline in her ability to care for herself. It also means she recognizes the limitations of her decision, is okay with the trade-offs, and knows she's saying "no" to another lifestyle—living in a small community with people her own age.

It's easiest to begin discussions with areas of agreement, which in this case are the positives of aging at home. You can agree about why seniors feel an increased comfort level in their own homes.

They can maintain established routines inside and outside the house.

There's an increased sense of autonomy and independent-minded-ness, perhaps affecting overall morale.

There's a familiarity and ease to handling visitors, whether it's family, friends, or strangers.

Their network or safety net is established (neighbors, nearby friends, health professionals, fix-it contacts).

There's even general agreement among professionals and non-professionals alike that after a health event, patients of all ages seem to heal better at home than in institutional settings.

It's likely that agreement can be reached on both comfort and familiarity, since these feelings draw on past and present emotions. More difficult, though, is the transition into topics regarding safety concerns and the future.

Safety at home concerns the addition of new people and new things, and my experience is that seniors often dislike both (new people and things) in their home unless they feel a part of the decision-making process. People and things represent change, and change is difficult for all of us, but especially for seniors. At this point in the discussion, whether or not your mother has a plan that supports her desire to stay home will be more obvious, but I think you'll find addressing "things" within the plan is easier than addressing "people."

Safety measures run the gamut, from limiting throw rugs (risk of tripping) to installing nightlights, from electrical wiring to surge protectors, from changing or eliminating nobs on stoves to lowering the height of shelves to ease access. These are small tweaks, and there are many more, that add major safety improvements.

Home security systems range from all-house protection to personal alert buttons that are worn in case of falls or acute health changes. Beyond the automatic first call to the central help desk, you can arrange to have the next call be either to you or to an emergency response team.

Home modifications—for instance, installing grab bars in the shower or by the commode, remodeling or adding a bathroom on the main floor, installing ramps or chair lifts where stairs exist—are often called retrofits. Retrofitting simply means you're adding new technology or features to an older design, changes that will ease completion of daily tasks, minimize safety concerns, and make floor plans more adaptable.

Clearly, the larger and more involved the changes are, the more expensive the decision will be. At the same time, however, the improvements will likely affect peace of mind spanning years of physical and mental changes—unknown, unpredictable, and bound to happen.

In terms of people coming into the home to help your loved one, change will typically occur somewhat gradually, but it may be the initial additions that are the most difficult to accept. Perhaps based on what you see is causing difficulty for your loved one, you may first attempt to hire help through a home healthcare agency, like I used for my mom, to handle setting up pill boxes, reordering medications, and interfacing with physicians to handle questions or concerns. Maybe it will be someone to cut grass, maintain flowers and shrubs, clean gutters, and shovel snow. Maybe you will decide to first address nutrition, cooking, and meal preparation, or you decide to look into housekeeping and/or handyman services. If personal care (bathing, dressing, meal preparation, feeding, and medication reminders) is particularly difficult, then you are likely looking for a home health aide, also known as a personal care aide or home care aide, whose time commitment can range from a few hours daily to live-in care. Whichever way you go, wherever you decide to begin the conversation, resistance and some degree of pushback should be expected.

Your conversation's overall success will depend on how thoroughly you understand your own family's structure, support system, and expectations. In other words, individual wishes and decisions are being addressed within a whole that is larger than just your immediate loved one(s). I've come to appreciate that there are many different family structures, ranging from those whose members are close geographically and emotionally, to those who are scattered geographically and absolutely non-committed emotionally, to every possible mix in between. In my dealings with seniors and their families, I've seen total caregiving services provided by a live-in family member, and I've also dealt with sons and daughters who live states away from their mother and father but hire and manage home services long distance. Either way can work well for extended periods or time or, occasionally, through end-of-life care.

It's possible, however, that even though you're hearing only about wishes to age in place at home, and you're helping to strengthen or facilitate a plan to make that happen, it may not be a solution that lasts forever. We cannot see the future and know the needs of years to come, whether that's with our mom, dad, or the family member caring for them. What we can do is address the present, make it as good as possible by adding changes that are needed now, and commit to handling the future needs as they arise.

We haven't yet addressed the biggest negative of aging at home which, depending on the age and overall health of your loved one, may not yet be a negative at all. If you're starting discussions early in your senior's life, then he/she is likely still involved with family, friends, and the community at large. However, the pool of contacts shrinks as people move or pass away, until suddenly you hear, "All my friends are gone." It's logical that the longer you stay in one place and call it "home," the better you know people and the more connected you feel. Imagine how sad you could feel when you think you're suddenly alone, because so many people you care about are no longer a part of your life. It can be overwhelming.

Feeling isolated is a key contributing factor to depression, which is massively under-diagnosed in the elderly; the flipside—socialization is often said to be "golden" for seniors missing contact with other people. But, ask yourself: what do isolated, lonely people often want to do when they're depressed and missing friends or the way life used to be? They want to cocoon and stay home, forever. The more they feel isolated, the more they want to stay home; it's almost as though by holding onto something familiar, they feel safe against the change that's happening around them.

If you find this scenario to be a part of your personal equation, then your solution will necessarily either be to bolster the stay-at-home option with conscious effort on creating or maintaining social connections, or you will need to begin sharing the benefits of more socialization in a new environment. While it may be up to you and your family to understand the situation and craft a solution, know that this dilemma is a key reason many families turn to the senior-living option for their loved ones. Just as isolation is the number-one negative of aging at home, so is socialization the number-one positive effect most often cited for senior community living.

At this point, many families have a similar idea: Why not have Mom move into our house and live with us? If you can get her to agree with the idea, which in some cases is not an easy task by itself, the combined family seems to generally work in most cases for some period of time. It certainly did for many generations before ours, right? But, we lead very different lives than people of generations gone by—much faster and more involved—and there's a huge hole in this solution that surprises everyone when they reach the point of needing (once again) to change the plan: Mom's alone all day, she's bored, she's unhappy. Actually, she's in a home that's not her home, surrounded by people she loves but whom she rarely sees, and she may be more unhappy than ever before. I'm not telling you to not do it if you want to try combined family living, but I am suggesting that I've rarely, if ever, seen it be more than a temporary stopgap. It's socialization and connectedness that are missing.

When I had one-on-one conversations with seniors considering senior community living, the loss of their close friends and family was often a major part of our talk. While they often liked the general idea of living near people with whom they shared similar life events, the thought of not knowing anyone and having to start all over was pretty scary. We often decided it was like being the new kid in school and dreading the lunchroom. We talked about senior communities often having a buddy system for new residents, whether official or not, and I often quickly put together a group of helpful residents with similar personalities to ease introductions to people, activities, and to talk about their own personal experiences becoming acclimated to a new lifestyle.

What I didn't share on a regular basis was that the community's seniors most reminded me of a much earlier time in my life when I arranged play dates for my toddler son, and we moms would talk about lengthy, peaceful chunks of time when "parallel play" ruled the time together. Sometimes there's not a lot of deep discussion happening, but they're still enjoying a pleasurable activity with someone else nearby. I thought of that often in the community dining room. Yet, there's the next step that's important: maybe an activity is scheduled immediately following the meal and everyone decides to go to Bingo, or the movie, or the tabletop bowling tournament, or they take the scheduled community minibus to the drugstore. Before they know it, they have shared experiences and their new "home" doesn't feel quite so new and strange.

Some of those relationships that seemed liked parallel play at the beginning were simply the beginning of a much stronger relationship that deepened over time. I can remember several dining tables for six or eight residents that were generally full of the same people, and I would see some of the same people together throughout the day, still enjoying the companionship and moving on to a different activity. Sometimes it was simply reading the newspaper or watching TV in the lounge, but they had a companion. I knew several women who initially bonded over playing card games, but they eventually invited some men into their games and things got interesting. Before long the group had expanded into board games and puzzles; they still played rowdy games of cards but also regularly shouted out suggestions to help solve a giant crossword puzzle on the wall. They became quite good at multi-tasking!

Occasionally, best friends develop, and while the majority of those friendships are between women, very occasionally a couple develops like Robert and Mary in chapter 3. Mary said to me more than once, "It makes me so mad that some people don't think we really love each other. Just because we're old, it doesn't mean we can't feel love just like we did when we were young." I agree. I'm not saying that you and I could find our own version of Robert and Mary when we're in our nineties, or that it will happen to whomever it is you love and are trying to help right now.

I am saying that it's not impossible, that relationships form in brand-new definitions of "home" when it seems scary and unlikely, and that believe it or not, it generally begins around being gathered together for the meals in the dining room.

Beyond new acquaintances, budding friendships, and activity options for your loved one to investigate, there are several other features of senior-living communities that will add to your peace of mind.

The difficult tasks surrounding homeownership are no longer an issue in community living. The building and apartment maintenance, beautification of the interior common areas and the exterior grounds, and small tasks like changing light bulbs or spot-cleaning carpets and upholstery are all taken care of by the staff. You don't have to do it for them or hire someone else to do it.

The nutrition issues, meal preparation, grocery shopping, and cooking concerns are a thing of the past. You can still bring your father his favorite homemade soup when you make a batch, or if you live close by, invite him over for Sunday suppers, birthday gatherings, and special events. Or you can eat with him in the community dining room (for a nominal charge). You don't have to worry about his eating, though, because there's staff that keeps an eye on your father's habits, his likes and dislikes, so you don't have food and nutrition worries.

Activity calendars for the month will offer a variety of options to keep your mother occupied throughout the day, and I've never met an activity director who didn't appreciate suggestions. In addition to the community's posted shopping trips and events outside the community, transportation also can be arranged to nearby doctor appointments, so driving there is no longer a problem. Additionally, most communities have doctors who visit routinely, so many residents no longer need to leave their home to attend scheduled appointments.

Communities take the safety of their residents very seriously; after all, you've entrusted them with the well-being of someone you love. There is staff available around the clock, including during nighttime, though that shift is covered with fewer staff members, and they tend to be more rotational than other shifts. The apartments are equipped or can be equipped with strategically located grab bars and a call system that alerts staff to emergency situations. In addition to having the comfort that someone will quickly answer your mother's needs, you will find yourself worrying less about strangers at her front door, extreme weather conditions, and environmental hazards like a nearby fire. The staff is trained with periodic drills covering a variety of situations.

Many of the best features of senior community living are all about minimizing stress, offering healthy options to overcome potential problems, and maximizing peace of mind for both seniors and their families. The best operations really care what you think and are open to your thoughts on how their community can improve.

One of the things I liked to talk about with families seriously considering the change to senior living is the expectation that everything will be perfect. It won't be . . . nothing is. But I could honestly guarantee that I would work as hard as I possibly could to get as close to "perfect" as they needed, and I always did. In addition to the renewed peace of mind that this lifestyle could bring to the family, I liked to share with them that it could also return a sense of normalcy to the family relationships. Without the scheduling of tasks and chores surrounding homeownership and the ever-necessary discussion of who's going to do whatever needs to be done, a visit can be more like a genuine visit. You suddenly realize that there's a gift of time involved, time that actually feels freer, more leisurely, and somehow more like days-gone-by. It can come unexpectedly, but it surely is a good feeling when it arrives.

For More Information

"Policy & Strategy Memorandum," National Aging in Place Council Annual Conference, Washington, D.C., June 9 – 10, 2014, accessed 6/25/2014,

http://www.ageinplace.org/Portals/0/NAIPC%20Policy%20Platform.pdf

Christy Rokoczy, "10 Reasons Home Care is Better Than Assisted Living," OpenPlacement Community Blog, November 19, 2013, accessed February 6, 2014,

https://www.openplacement.com/community/blog/
reasons-why-home-care-better-assisted-living.

Joanna Saison and Monika White, "Home Care Services for Seniors: Services to Help You Stay at Home," Helpguide.org, February 2014 (last updated), accessed March 29, 2014,

http://www.helpguide.org/elder/senior_services_living_home.htm.

Lawrence Robinson, Joanna Saisan, and Monika White, "Senior Housing Options: assess your needs and make the best senior living/residential care choice," Helpguide. org, February 2014 (last updated), accessed March 29, 2014,

http://www.helpguide.org/elder/senior_housing_residential_care_types.htm.

Christy Rokoczy, 10 Reasons Assisted Living is Better Than Home Care," OpenPlacement Community Blog, November 13, 2013, accessed February 6, 2014,

https://www.openplacement.com/community/blog/
reasons-why-assisted-living-better-home-care/.

CHAPTER TWELVE

Going Forward

You're finally to the point where the tough discussions, pulling together dispersed information, holding family meetings, and shaping a directional plan are all moving from the to-do list to something more actionable. You may not have a final decision yet about which of the two main choices—at-home care or community living—will ultimately be decided upon, but that's actually a good place to pause until some investigations have been made. Let the discussions rest while you continue talking with some people in both camps . . . and maybe have a talk with yourself about expectations.

Let's say you're trying to help your mom and dad and are investigating long-term care options on their behalf. Here's the problem that faces all of us when we try to help facilitate the last chapter for those we love. We think in terms of shaping their future into something that's as limited and manageable as possible so they can control it easily when their health declines. The path we're trying to help them shape and control, though, is one that's fluid, unpredictable, and actually completes itself over the years to come. We want maximum ease, safety, and happiness for them, which is a pretty nice wish. But, no matter how well we tidy up their path, no matter how satisfied, grateful, and pleased they seem, it just doesn't last forever . . . because time and change march on.

Life changes, health declines in unsuspected ways, and different needs result, but it's through no fault of theirs or ours! It's simply life, the last chapter of life, and it's out of our control. The perfect scenario today may suddenly turn into the poorest fit imaginable, and you may find yourself wondering, What was I thinking? How could I ever think this (house, apartment, staff, personal help) would work? I'll wager it did work, it was a good fit for a while, but life just happened to turn it upside down. Try to be easy on yourself.

If and when unforeseen change happens regarding the housing plan you've facilitated, you'll do what we all do: pick up the pieces, smooth things over, return to files of notes, and start again. You'll make calls, search on the Internet, interview or re-interview people, revisit options, and bring your mom or dad into the equation as much as possible. You have more information this time or, more likely, a different set of needs that have been presented by an acute health event.

One of the more common but nevertheless painful situations is this: the family house was retrofitted for your mother or father to remain at home, terrific help was found, everything was working beautifully, and then one of the parents passes away suddenly. For a variety of reasons and, hopefully, with an agreed-upon decision, the family is now looking at senior community living for the remaining parent. Was the stay-at-home decision wrong? Absolutely not. It was the best decision at the time based on the facts at hand and the expressed wishes of the parties involved. However, now it's different. Life has changed, and you rally to do the best you can all over again. The path can suddenly take a turn, but the point is that you can only do the best you can do at that particular time.

Even though the journey you're helping facilitate is fluid and unpredictable, the options within the continuum of care for your loved one are fairly stagnant. Once you get the lay of the land and understand the mix of jargon, you'll be on your way to productivity. Labels can be confusing at first, and just when you think you have a handle on it, you confront a new twist on an old term. Most of the time, however, you can relax; instead of a new creation, it's simply someone trying to sound fancy. My preference is always to learn the basics, and then you can recognize fluff—or a truly new innovation— when you come across it.

Within the full spectrum of long-term care options, the starting point for all options is going to be the "home" wherever your loved one is today. It may be the family homestead you've known for decades, the home where you grew up, or the house where you visited your grandparents. It may be a condo, townhouse, or apartment that was the initial attempt at downsizing. Your starting point could even be within a senior community that no longer meets the needs of your loved one. Whatever the situation, you see a need to insert more care into the current situation, thereby changing "home" from the way it is currently functioning. Whether you're able to tack on additional interventions at the current location or you need to change "home" to a completely new address, a continuum of care for aging seniors generally addresses incremental help for declining abilities. The help may be temporary or permanent, and you can always change your decision as events and health dictate.

Your goal is to get it right, to make the choices that truly fit your need, and if or when you find out the "fit" just isn't what you thought it was going to be, then you may need to cut your losses and move on. If you happen to be an individual who is a perfectionist about life, then you'll probably be frustrated in your pursuit of getting it right and keeping it right. But remember the life and times of Leigh caring for her uncle Robert in chapter 3: you do what you have to do at each new juncture.

In the sections ahead, and from the starting point of your loved one's current "home," we'll look at options for at-home care that allow them to remain where they currently live. We'll take a look at augmenting your loved one's success at living in their home with help from both trained people and remarkably unobtrusive technology. Then we'll look specifically at the different variations of senior living communities, who they best serve, plus the strengths and limitations of each. And even though the Internet makes it infinitely easier than it was years ago to gather information about choices on the spectrum of care, you will still get to the point when you must tour communities and interview personnel. You'll discover who's really in charge, what to look for and why, plus information and questions to personalize for your particular circumstances. You will be better informed and more empowered to meet the challenges of the winding road ahead of you, and you'll be headed in the right direction to do the best you can do.

SECTION FOUR

Aging in Place with Additional Care

CHAPTER THIRTEEN

The Decision to Age at Home

If you are pursuing options to augment aging in place at home, then we have to assume it is the wish of the aging senior in your life. You may not have perfect agreement from all parties involved that this is the best solution, but the decision has been reached that "home" will remain Home for as long as it continues to be safe and maximizes day-to-day living. You may have arrived at this spot through some messy discussions, but you can breathe once again and start to take actions that will help make the home situation function better than it does today.

Key components to the decision were likely familiarity with the neighborhood, people (family, friends, neighbors), and businesses (stores, healthcare professionals, churches). You believe transportation is easily accessible, at least through some combination of friends, family, and neighbors. We're also assuming that the neighborhood is safe, especially for seniors, and the home is in good repair; perhaps modifications have been made to make life easier, safer, or to address changing needs (wheelchair ramp, security or emergency response system, bathtub railings, nightlights). Perhaps rooms have even been repurposed to create a first-floor bedroom, or a new bathroom has been added. Most likely, we can also assume your loved one's physical, mental, and medical needs do not require a high level of care, and at the same time their mobility is still reasonably good. In essence, you believe that if you hire people to help with personal care and to do the things around the house that need to be done, then the bridge created by those hired helpers will be accepted by your mother, father, or whoever you're trying to help stay at home.

What's next can be broken down into two parts. Step One is totally actionable and needs to consume your efforts: find the caregivers. Create the bridge you think will span the gap that keeps the at-home environment from being what it needs to be. Find the people who can make the aging-at-home experience as close to perfect as it can reasonably be, who can not only get the task done, but who can also do it in such a way that respect, independence, happiness, and satisfaction are a part of every day. Find caregivers who can communicate, who are not simply about completing the job, but who want to get to know the person you love. Find the type of caregiver who can restore peace of mind for your loved one and for you. There will be trial and error, but the caregivers you want and need are out there, waiting to be found. The first step is completely actionable and finite: caregivers will be hired, schedules arranged, and care completed in the arranged timeframe. If the personalities don't mesh, then you make adjustments; but there's a beginning, middle, and end to this step.

Step Two is not as neat. In order for this to work, there has to be acceptance by your loved one of the new bridge you helped them build. This part is largely beyond your control, and all you can actually do is to knock yourself out doing the best you can on Step One. Maybe you'll be one of the lucky ones who receive thankfulness and obvious pleasure in return for your hard work putting stellar caregivers in place. But if acceptance doesn't come, you can explain, reiterate, remind, restate, and coach all parties involved until you're blue in the face; you just can't dial-in an attitude change.

Sometimes, the person you love may approve of the help you've added to the equation; they may even agree with the need for help. Despite that, though, the bottom line can still be they don't like the invasiveness of having new people in their private space, and that's a tough one. There can be a lot of frustration as we live with their behaviors, especially if and when the behaviors follow an exacting execution of what we thought was the plan they wanted. I could tell you what did not work for me when I was helping my parents and Dad was so sick, but you will develop your own means of massaging a less than ideal attitude, some of which may work and some that don't. Remember, though, that the core of the question, "Who are we?" is not the experience I had or the one you will have; it's the answer to the question: We are the primary caregivers and all that it entails, even the most difficult of situations. I hope for you the changes you implement will be accepted, but you are not alone if difficulties prevail.

CHAPTER FOURTEEN

At-home Care

The terminology used for help at home always confused me. In my mind, it was lumped together under "home care." It's actually carefully separated into the two labels, non-medical care and home health care, the latter implying but not stating that it is the medical half of the two groups. For example, when I started hiring help with my mom's prescription medicine, I learned that states require an R.N. for order/re-ordering medication, interfacing with doctors or other nurses regarding medication changes or questions, and pill set-up for the week. This set of tasks then becomes slightly more expensive than, say, the nursing aides who perform the medication "reminders" when it's time for the client to take their pills; however, the two separate sets of duties will generally be combined under "medication management." By using a full service home healthcare agency, the confusion in labels gradually went away for me because they simply put the appropriate personnel in place for the task at hand.

You'll find home care (non-medical) help provides professional caregivers. This means caregiving is their profession, but not necessarily that they have additional education and licensing. They help in the home (house, condo, apartment, senior community) and assist with bathing, dressing, preparing meals, eating, and cleaning. Sometimes you can arrange a morning service (bathing, dressing, eating breakfast, taking medications) and/or a bedtime service (medications, help undressing, safely getting to bed) or staying overnight. It's also possible to extend hours for companionship, which sometimes is equally or more important than physical help with tasks throughout the day.

Home health care provides medically related services in the home (house, condo, apartment, senior community) instead of in a medical facility (hospital, nursing home). You will have medically trained and licensed individuals, such as physical and occupational therapists, speech therapists, or skilled nursing, who will help increase the ability to tend to one's own needs. These services are provided in response to a doctor's prescription for a limited timeframe and can also include post-operative care, wound care, mobility training, pain management, intravenous therapy, and injections. Home healthcare providers can only perform the prescribed tasks, and then their time with your loved one is done.

You can find both home care (non-medical) and home healthcare (medical) through a full service home healthcare agency, and even though it may be a pricier option, background checks and confirmation of credentials have already been completed for you. Since the caregiver works for the agency, taxes and billing will be handled by the employer, as well as protections for you regarding theft and quick replacement of caregivers if things don't work out.

Let's look at the non-medical help you may want to first locate to bolster life at home. We have talked about the many reasons why seniors want to age in place, one of the main reasons being their comfort level with already established networks of friends, family, and business contacts. This is exactly where you will want to begin looking for the help you need. The people you already know, or the people you have access to through people you know, will be your greatest source of trusted referrals. Perhaps the contacts themselves will be interested in helping, but even if they aren't, they may have personal experience in hiring the same type of skills you happen to be seeking. Or, they may have a friend who hired someone who worked out perfectly. Now is the time to leverage the contacts that made the "home" feel so secure and safe. People know people . . . you just have to ask.

If you're looking for non-medical help—say, help with the yard, housekeeping, laundry, transportation, or getting meals together— friends, family, and neighbors should be a good source of information. Consider checking with church or synagogue members, colleagues at work, and doctors or other healthcare professionals for help with personal care. Also, think in terms of combined responsibilities and opportunities: if you're looking for a driver, it's ideal if the person you find to drive to the doctor or grocery store realizes the job may also include trips to a weekly bridge group or regularly scheduled knitting or quilting groups. Maybe the person you find to help with laundry and housekeeping is pretty good at playing Gin Rummy or some other game your father enjoys, and if the personalities mesh, it's a great way to spend time together. The more fluid and non-task-oriented you can make it, the more home-like and "normal" it will seem.

If you find yourself needing referral possibilities beyond those from people you know, then try searching online for older adult resources. You'll look for comprehensive listings that include local area agencies on aging, senior centers, and eldercare resources. A solid starting place is the National Eldercare Locator by the US Administration on Aging (Department of Health and Human Services), which has links to local area agencies on aging and community-based services. The search within the site is based on either your zip code or city/state or by topic from a drop-down box (but not location and topic at the same time). The resources are varied and will point you in the right direction for more information.

A more comprehensive online site is Elder Care Resources: Information for an Aging World (www.eldercareresourcesusa.com). The landing page requires clicking on the state for which you are gathering information (say, www.eldercareresourcesillinois.com), which in turn opens to an enormous amount of information. The button bar includes finding a home care provider, resources (national, state, general, legal), caregiver education, expert advice (short videos by topic), blogs, and free downloads. I particularly like this site because of its breadth of topics that reach some of the more difficult areas of being either the primary caregiver or a caregiver in general.

The search beyond your personal network of acquaintances will quickly take you into the world of home healthcare providers, which, like any business category, runs the gamut from excellent to barely reputable. Licensed home healthcare providers are regulated by individual states' Department of Health and are subject to both scheduled and unannounced inspections. Governed by federal, state, and local laws, their licensure is subject to strict compliance with standards regarding state boards of medicine, nursing, pharmacy, physical therapy, and occupational therapy. Other areas of compliance may include standards concerning communicable and non-communicable diseases, controlled substances, drugs, and equipment or devices. When the State arrives for an agency review, it is a multiple day affair: thorough, stressful, and with possible mandated remediation, fines, or in extreme situations, suspension of their agency license.

There are several ways to begin searching for a home healthcare agency to help your loved one. Doctors and nurses are always good sources of referrals, especially if you ask ones who have recently treated the individual you're helping and who are familiar with their current needs. Beyond their general practitioner (GP), ask any physician specialists involved in their recent care. If your loved one has had a recent health event putting them in the hospital or nursing home for rehabilitation, you'll probably receive a prescription at discharge for home-care services, so ask what agency they would recommend.

Alternatively, if there has been no health event and you just want to explore options, consider calling a nearby senior living community and ask for either the sales and marketing director or the director of nursing (who will likely be harder to reach). Explain the situation to them, including your decision to support efforts for your loved one to age at home, and ask whom they would consider hiring if it were their Mom, Dad, or whomever. I've received many calls like this and can attest to always having an opinion based on agency performance in my building. Residents and their families would often come to me to talk about both positive and negative experiences with the personnel who helped them, so even though you're not looking to be a part of a senior community at this time, the sources of information are still worth investigating.

There are two additional ideas that might be extremely helpful if your loved one lives in the right geography to take advantage of the programs. The Village concept and Naturally Occurring Retirement Communities (NORCs) are two separate, similar but yet different programs that allow seniors to age at home with help. The programs supply personnel to help seniors when help is needed; both are economical and proven solutions, but neither has achieved national coverage despite solid growth. The limiting factor for both is that they have developed more extensively in metropolitan areas than beyond.

The Village concept opened in 2002 with a group of Boston seniors (Beacon Hill Village) who wanted to stay in their homes as they aged. They wanted to be responsible, knew they needed help, but didn't want to become dependent on their children; perhaps most of all, they wanted to stay at home, surrounded by the culture and friends they loved, rather than move to a "cookie-cutter retirement home." Beacon Hill Village became the first grass-roots, non-profit membership organization to provide free or low cost services to seniors living in their homes. Today, its membership has grown to more than four hundred members, all of whom live within the boundaries of two long-established neighborhoods.

Membership fees (2014: $675 per year for individual; $975 per household), volunteers, and fundraising remain the foundation of their services. Separate foundations subsidize membership for neighbors with incomes below $45,000 per year. Members benefit from free or dis-counted (10%–50%) services as needed: health and wellness programs, social and cultural events, discounts to vetted service providers, help managing their household, and transportation. Additional income from the creation of a manual explaining the Beacon Hill business model, along with structured consulting fees, has strengthened member services and helped other communities replicated the Village concept.

Today, more than 150 Villages exist across the country, each formed and governed locally but tailored to the specific needs of the commu-nity. The end result in each case is that there are flexible and affordable services available to members who have made the decision to age at home with help as needed. Services can range from minimal to exten-sive. Community-based service models have tremendous appeal to Baby Boomers as they continue to age and assess their options for projected years of declining health—both for themselves and for the loved ones they find themselves assisting. Find out more about the Village concept and their locations at Village to Village Network: http://vtvnetwork.org.

Another support system for aging in place, Naturally Occurring Retirement Communities (NORCs) have evolved in communities, neigh-borhoods, single-family housing developments, apartment buildings, and in other areas with high concentrations of older residents who have aged together. First identified in the mid-1980s in metropolitan areas, NORCs—also known as NORC Supportive Services Program, NORC-SSPs, or just SSPs—now exist is cities, small towns, and even some rural areas throughout the United States. The exact number of fully functioning NORC-SSPs varies widely, but all estimates claim there are thousands; at the same time, highly concentrated, definable areas of seniors continue to evolve.

NORCs' operational support is a mix of public and private funding: subsidies from federal, state, and local governments, housing partners, philanthropies, charities, corporations, and local businesses. Their goal is to increase the health, well-being, and security of seniors who want to live independently and age at home, and, by meeting their goal with seniors, to strengthen the overall health of the community at large.

The first NORC-SSP, a ten-building housing cooperative in New York City, was established in 1986 with support from the UJA (United Jewish Appeal)/Federation of New York, known as the world's largest local philanthropy. Since then, the first New York location has become the model for more than twenty-five states, and it services more than 50,000 seniors in forty-plus SSPs in New York State alone. Local program offerings are determined by the needs of the seniors and their community but include case management and social work services, healthcare management and nursing services, education, socialization, and recreation activities, community engagement, ancillary services (housekeeping, transportation, adult day programs, mental health counseling, legal advice, and more as determined locally). To find out more about Naturally Occurring Retirement Communities, their history, and what may be available in your area, see NORCS: An Aging in Place Initiative: https://www.norcs.org.

For More Information

Christina Morales, "Need to Hire an In Home Care Agency? 10 Questions You Should Ask Them," OpenPlacement Community Blog, August 12, 2014, accessed August 13, 2014

https://www.openplacement.com/community/blog/
need-hire-in-home-care-agency-10-questions-ask/.

Joanna Saison and Monika White, "Home Care Services for Seniors: Services to Help You Stay at Home," Helpguide.org, February 2014 (last updated), accessed March 29, 2014

http://www.helpguide.org/elder/senior_services_living_home.htm.

Alyssa Chan, "Senior Care – A Detailed Look," OpenPlacement Community Blog, December 18, 2013, accessed April 8, 2014

https://www.openplacement.com/community/blog/senior-care/.

Mary Jo Brooks, "How One Group of Seniors Bucked Convention and Avoided the Retirement Home," PBS NewsHour, August 8, 2013

http://www.programsforelderly.com/homecare-beacon-hill-village.php

Beacon Hill Village, accessed April 1, 2014

http://www.beaconhillvillage.org.

Village to Village Network, accessed April 1, 2014

http://www.vtvnetwork.org.

Amanda Lehning, Joan Davitt, Andrew Scharlach, and Emily Greenfield, "Village Sustainability and Engaging a Diverse Membership: Key Findings from a 2013 National Survey," University of Maryland, School of Social Work, Village to Village Network, accessed April 1, 2014

https://vtvnetwork.clubexpress.com.

NORCs: An Aging in Place Initiative, accessed February 4, 2015

https://www.norcs.org/norc-paradigm/

"History of The Jewish Federations of North America's Aging in Place Initiative, NORCs: An Aging in Place Initiative," accessed February 4, 2015

http://www.norcs.org/

CHAPTER FIFTEEN

Technology

You're probably somewhat like I am: we maintain a level of awareness regarding many of technology's advancements in cell phones, computers, televisions, and the ever-changing offerings by various providers of data packages powering the devices—but all at arm's length. We're bombarded by information about all the advances in tech products and are assured we absolutely need the latest and greatest gadget right now. I usually don't respond until I decide my old one's broken and I need a new one. Then I go searching for what fits my needs at the time.

This may be a reasonable analogy to where you are right now. You feel like you're bending over backward, trying to make things work well to accommodate a safe, fulfilling chapter in aging at home, but you're missing something to complete the equation. Maybe you live miles or states away from your loved one and can't check in with them for a face-to-face visit on a regular basis. Maybe you do everything you can to facilitate their regular doctor appointments, but it's increasingly taxing on them and difficult for you to schedule time off from work. Maybe you wonder if they're really taking their blood pressure, blood glucose, or monitoring their vitals as regularly as they claim to be, or maybe you're worried about the likelihood of more falls. If any or all of these are true, then maybe your old methods of gathering enough information are no longer fully functioning and you need a new way. Telemedicine, a relatively new means of making homes safer for seniors wishing to age in place, may offer you the solution you're seeking. It may even give you more accurate information, save you time and trips to the doctor, and provide a safety measure that feels exceptionally welcome.

My first exposure to telemedicine was in its very early, formative years when there wasn't much more to it than a call system. Clients had a choice between a pendant necklace and a pendant on a watch-like strap that they would wear every day and press during an emergency. Assuming they were relatively near their monitoring device, their emergency call would be answered by a warm and friendly voice: "Ellen, this is Your Home Alert Company, how can I help you?" My mom had a full-service system set up for free in her apartment. Our community only had emergency pull-cords in the bath and bedroom, so I used Mom's apartment to show an example of systems residents could incorporate to expand their safety zone. It also detected a lack of regularly timed movement in the apartment, so if subscribers weren't up and moving an hour after their usual get-up time in the morning, the company would start making calls for a safety check on their behalf.

There were occasionally a few problems with the system, but overall it seemed pretty advanced at the time. Major providers of this type of emergency monitoring still advertise on television, so the systems are still available and, I assume, are now without some of the early kinks we experienced. However, based on my experience with them and exposure to seniors using them, I believe the trouble is not with the systems themselves but with the customers who wear the devices. My mom gave me a first-hand example that was added to by numerous other seniors in the community: they fell, but they forgot they were wearing the emergency pendant. Sometime after Mom's fall and the resulting broken hip, I asked her why she didn't use her emergency pendant to call for help. She said, "Well, I just put it on and wear it every day, and I forgot what it was for." And so went the same story from family members of other residents in peril. They wore it but forgot its use.

I also had exposure to the early stages of the more advanced telemedicine, which is a completely different product and considerably more sophisticated than the early gadgets I'm describing. I saw telemedicine save lives. At the time, our assisted-living floor was augmented by a full-service home healthcare agency that was consistently up to date with the latest advances in the medical and home health industries. They supplied a device that looked like a flat weight scale for the residents to step onto each morning, but each device was programmed to send clinical data through the residents' telephones to a monitoring center and tele-nursing. Several of our residents were in advanced stages of congestive heart failure and, because of excessive water-weight gain overnight (which is a signal of impending heart failure), they were rushed to the hospital in time to save their life.

Telehealth, which is broader in scope than telemedicine, can be life saving for seniors with health issues who nevertheless want to age at home. Home telehealth service and monitoring requires a doctor's approval. In addition to the telecommunication technologies used to transmit remote clinical data, it also provides non-clinical services like training and education to both providers and the end users. Seniors can use their tele-monitoring device and their phone to reach a nurse (24 hours a day/365 days a year) to be reminded of routines, ask a question, or receive supportive but specific counseling. Anecdotally, there are many stories about senior telehealth users taking an increased interest in their own health as they learn to monitor themselves and learn lifelong self-management routines. Improved patient outcomes become noticeable as they make important changes to their lives, are encouraged by the patient-specific telehealth support they receive, and are able to reduce trips to the doctor, the emergency room, and costly hospitalizations.

Technology being what it is, monitoring devices helpful to seniors have exploded in the number of options available and have splintered into many separate small companies. Their offerings, generally known as "wearables," bring a variety of services to the market. Systems can monitor cardiac issues, falls, missed medications or meals, lack of movement, and much more. My favorite new device brings hope to those of you fearing your loved one will wander away from home and become lost, afraid, or injured before they're located: a GPS embedded insole tracks the location of your loved one . . . welcome to a new age! A few of the newer websites are listed in "More Information" to get you started on your research.

As you look for ways to increase support needed for successful aging in place at home, using new tech devices may be the missing link for you and your loved one. If you investigate more about monitoring systems and decide it's a real possibility for your situation, know that many home healthcare agencies and physician groups are familiar with the latest options and can supply you with information about the appropriate devices. You can add questions about healthcare monitoring system and the newest "wearables" to your growing list for interviewing agencies and finding the agency and/or device you think best fits your situation and your loved one's needs.

For More Information

"What is telehealth? How is telehealth different from telemedicine?" HealthIT.gov, March 21, 2014, accessed October 7, 2014

www.healthit.gov/providers-professionals/faqs/
what-telehealth-how-telehealth-different-telemedicine

Elaine Pofeldt, "Telemedicine Keeps Seniors Out of Nursing Homes," Special to CNBC. com, January 14, 2014, accessed October 7, 2014

https://www.cnbc.com/id/101316376.

Audrey Kinsella, Guide to Long Term Care Planning: About Home Telehealth," National Care Planning Council, accessed October 6, 2014

https://www.longtermcarelink.net/eldercare/home_telehealth.htm

"What is Telemedicine?" American Telemedicine Association, accessed October 6, 2014

http://www.americantelemed.org.

"Using Telemedicine to Care for Aging Parents," Pro Connections, accessed March 27, 2014

http://www.rockawave.com/news/2015-06-05/Columnists/Telemedicine_and_Care_
Giving_for_the_Aging.html

Steve Moran, "A Perspective on Emergency Call Systems and Senior Housing Technology," Senior Housing Forum, February 10, 2013, accessed March 26, 2014

seniorhousingforum.net/blog/2013/2/10/
perspective-emergency-call-systems-and-senior-housing-technology

Kristen Hicks, "What is Wearable Technology?" SeniorAdvisor.com, accessed May 3, 2015

https://www.senioradvisor.com/blog/2015/01/what-is-wearable-technology/.

Preventice, accessed May 3, 2015

http://www.preventice.com.

BeClose, accessed May 3, 2015

http://www.beclose.com.

Lively Safety Watch and In-Home Activity Sensors, accessed May 3, 2015

http://www.mylively.com.

GPS Smart Sole, accessed May 3, 2015

http://www.gpssmartsole.com.

CHAPTER SIXTEEN

Continuum of Care

No matter which road you're traveling, whether you're supporting your loved one's decision to age in place at home or you've found them wanting to explore senior community living, eventually there will come a time when a health event changes the carefully crafted lay of the land. It doesn't matter whether you're just starting to help or they're completely settled in their new "home"; you will look back later on their crisis and see that life changed at that moment. There's never a good time for a frightening health event, but it somehow seems to come at the worst possible times and with more complications than can be imagined beforehand.

The health event could arrive on the heels of a completed move to the new apartment in a chosen community (I saw this several times, including with my own mom). Or it could happen midway on a long cross-country flight when the senior's crisis forces the plane to make an emergency landing in a strange city (this happened to a friend's parents). Or the health event could take place when you're two days out to sea on your first cruise (this happened with another friend's mother). Not only are you dealing with the horrors and fears of the crisis itself, but more than likely there are personal complications that make everything even more dramatic.

We can't predict the "what," "when," or the "where" of the health events that will change your life, but what we can address is the similarity of the places the event will take you as you follow the path of recovery. We can demystify some of the language and look at the rather limited purposes of each location. The continuum of care following a health event includes hospitals, nursing homes, and sub-acute care; the goal is always to return the injured party to the life they were leading prior to the health event. That's why I say that it doesn't matter what decisions have been made or which ones are in process to maximize what "home" is going to be. If the event happens to your mother in the house you grew up in and you're midway through retrofitting, or if Uncle John is adapting to a new apartment he seemingly likes in a senior community, it really doesn't matter. After a health event, the continuum of care will likely begin with entrance to a hospital through the emergency room.

Hospitals are the most restrictive environment with the highest level of care. They are designed to meet all of the medical needs of a critically ill patient. Their staff is in charge of the patient, not the other way around (much to the dismay of many seniors). Physician and nursing services provide diagnoses and medical or surgical treatment twenty-four hours a day to patients who are acutely ill, accident victims, among others. Some hospitals provide treatment for mental illness, while most provide testing and minor medical procedures or treatments in special inpatient centers within their facilities or in satellite offices.

A patient's length of stay in the hospital is generally shorter than family expects. You and I look at the person in the hospital bed and measure what we see against the way they normally function day to day. Our analysis tells us they have a long way to go and need to stay where they are. Hospitals, on the other hand, monitor specific criteria measuring whether or not the patient's needs require their acute care services; when sufficient progress has been made, discussions regarding discharge will take place. Your head may swim with all of the reasons why your mother isn't yet ready to go home, but they're probably not talking about a discharge to home. They're probably going to discharge her to a nursing home or sub-acute care.

The first time this happened to me, I panicked. Place Mom in a nursing home? No, no, no . . . she has her own apartment in a retirement complex and would never agree to a nursing home. Fortunately, hospitals have become more consumer-friendly over the years and do a much better job than they once did explaining their decisions and offering options.

Hospitals usually talk about discharge to a facility other than a hospital that is able to provide both medical and rehabilitative care in the same setting. The patients may still require skilled nursing care and therapy to return to their former level of functioning. Many hospitals have created a wing or floor that functions as a skilled nursing home, also known as sub-acute or post-acute care, to take the patient through the early stages of care following hospitalization for an acute health event.

Other than the hospitals with their own distinct area for medical and rehabilitation services, there are also rehabilitative hospitals and skilled nursing facilities that are primarily freestanding. Patients have the necessary bedside nursing care, plus they travel by wheelchair to a separate area for physical, occupational, and/or speech therapy. Any activity beyond staying in bed is classified as therapeutic, such as dressing themselves, going to the bathroom by themselves, and even eating their meals in a chair by their bed or in a dining room with other recovering patients.

Time in this specialized hospital unit generally ends one of two ways: either a discharge to home or to an outside sub-acute care facility. For example, after one of Mom's congestive heart failure episodes, she spent a few weeks rehabbing in the hospital's own skilled nursing facility and then was discharged to her own apartment. Another time, following surgery for a broken hip, she spent multiple weeks in her original hospital room, a week or so on the hospital's skilled nursing floor, and then was discharged to an outside skilled nursing home for a month of extensive therapy. This was the same hospital for both events, but the different events resulted in different care plans. Nevertheless, some of the same bumpy patches in the road to recovery appeared both times and were a little unnerving.

Hospital personnel will tell you that one of the big advantages of having an in-hospital skilled nursing home is that the patients don't have to become confused by changing locations. That's not really true, at least for the seniors I've known. Remember Relocation Stress Syndrome, also known as Transfer Trauma, from chapter 4? My personal adage is that there's no such thing as a good move for a senior. It doesn't matter if it's across the hall, across town, the state or the country; it's still confusing, and there will be resulting behaviors. At the hospital, when you're told that using their rehab services will lessen the confusion as compared to patients transferring to an outside location, you can remain skeptical. If you believe in Relocation Stress and Transfer Trauma, then it follows that if there's a difference in their personal space, immediate surroundings, people, and routines, then it doesn't really matter if it's under the same roof. Expect confusion and, if your loved one is like my mom, some attitude.

Mom didn't really feel well enough to travel to the patients' dining room and socialize while eating, but the nurses insisted she needed her therapy. She complained her dinner partners fell asleep in their soup, didn't talk anyway, so why couldn't she eat alone? She made it clear she didn't like sharing her "apartment" with her new roommate, who was actually a hospital patient just like herself, and wanted to move to another senior community. There was a pattern peculiar to my mom that she and I struggled with every time a health event took her away from her own apartment and into a hospital setting: she was always operating on the schedule of the location she had just left. She was consistent, but in her mind she was one location behind. When she moved from the hospital to an outside skilled nursing home for a several weeks of therapy, her questions told me that she was picturing the hospital routine. Later, when she eventually came home to her own apartment following a month of therapy at the nursing home for her hip, she adhered to the routines and schedule of the nursing home. Instead of arriving for lunch and dinner in the community dining room, which was her home-base routine, she showed up for all three meals because that had been her pattern for four weeks in the nursing home. This is a little unsettling. If you see similar behavior, just know that it normally works itself out in a few days with some gentle reminding.

You might also see some other behaviors surface. I remember two calls from the head of the therapy unit regarding Mom's poor behavior and snippy attitude toward her. She wondered if Mom was usually this difficult. When asked to explain further, the director said Mom was doing the exercises but was complaining about the therapists being condescending and "talking down" to her, which she assured me she wasn't doing. Relieved that Mom was actually completing the exercises necessary to get stronger, I felt I could more freely answer the attitude question. "Yes," I admitted, "Mom's got a nose for sniffing out condescension. She was an elementary music teacher for twenty-five years and prided herself on never talking down to her students."

It didn't surprise me at all that this attitude was showing up, especially when Mom was in the role of student. Quite frankly, it never improved. I talked with Mom a couple of times about trying to be a little nicer to the therapists, but it only seemed to worsen her behavior; after all, she felt the director had "ratted" her out to me and should have kept her mouth shut. I did, however, draw a firm line with Mom against slapping away the therapist's hand, even though Mom felt she being shown some simplistic motion to perform and being talked down to at the same time. The director appreciated that I was trying to work with Mom toward improved behavior, and since Mom wasn't going to be a long-term resident, the therapists agreed to suck it up and stop trying to fit Mom into the "ideal patient" mold.

The good news about nursing homes, sub-acute care, and restorative care is that it is a component of Medicare Part A. Skilled Nursing Facility Benefits is part of the hospital insurance provided with Medicare, as long as the patient has an acute care hospital stay of three days or more and still requires daily skilled nursing care or rehabilitation services. If that is true, then the beneficiary is eligible for up to 100 days of skilled nursing home care. Medicare will cover the first 21 days at 100 percent and the remaining days at 80 percent. Coordination with Medicare-approved supplemental insurance will normally result in full coverage for days 21–100, making this level of care available to many beneficiaries at no out-of-pocket expense to them. By all means have a discussion on the day of admission, or prior if it's possible, with the billing department at the location where your loved one will be receiving services. The stay will generate an inordinate amount of paperwork, which, if you're the Financial Power of Attorney, you'll receive. Even though facility personnel will be available as questions arise, it's always a good idea to clarify things at the beginning and begin to establish a relationship.

Almost without exception when the skilled nursing home providing therapy services approaches their final discharge planning, they will make a sales presentation to try to convince you of the benefits of permanent placement for your loved one with them. The reasoning will go something like this. "We can provide you with everything in one place. With an apartment right here for your uncle Jim, he has on-site access to doctors, nurses, therapists, and all the meals and social activities he enjoyed while he was with us. Wouldn't it make your life so much simpler if he were here?" That's a decision you'll have to make on your own, but just be forewarned that the discussion is coming.

The majority of the nursing homes I've been exposed to are either newer construction or heavily rehabbed older ones, nicely decorated, and a very expensive proposition. However, most of them also include a limited number of Medicaid beds, which may or may not be available since demand is so high. If this approach to residency plus medical and therapeutic services makes sense to you, then prepare your list of questions in pursuit of it, but be certain of two things: (1) your uncle Jim agrees with you, and (2) you fully understand the flexibility of other options like assisted living, which is half the cost of a nursing home. Just be certain you have toured extensively and have ruled out choices for sound, solid reasons.

For More Information

Alyssa Chan, "Senior Care – A Detailed Look," OpenPlacement Community Blog, December 18, 2013, accessed April 8, 2014

https://www.openplacement.com/community/blog/senior-care/.

Dan Trigub, "Improving the Patient Experience in the Hospital," OpenPlacement Community Blog, October 9, 2014, accessed October 10, 2014

https://www.openplacement.com/communityblog/ improving-the-patient-experience-in-the-hospital/.

Curaspan Health Group with Mark Lachs, M.D., "The Growing Disconnect Between Hospitals and Post-Acute Providers," June 7, 2011, accessed October 10, 2014

http://www.kevinmd.com/blog/2011/06/growing-disconnect-hospitals-postacute-providers.html

Catherine H. Messick, "Subacute Care," University of Texas Health Science, San Antonio, accessed October 3, 2014

geriatrics.uthscsa.edu/tools/subacute_snf_care.pdf.

"Genworth 2013 Cost of Care Survey," Genworth Financial Inc. and National Eldercare Referral Systems, LLC

http://www.genworth.com.

Jordan Grumet, MD, "Nursing Homes: Our Society Has Chosen to See Only Darkness," KevinMD.com., October 8, 2014, accessed October 10, 2014

http://www.kevinmd.com/blog/2014/10/nursing-homes-society-chosen-see-darkness.html.

"The Nursing Home Checklist"

www.medicare.gov/NHCompare.

Samuel Brody, M.D. and Jane K. Brody, R.N., Voice of Experience: Stories about Health Care and the Elderly, by Samuel Brody and Jane K. Brody, 2012.

CHAPTER SEVENTEEN

The Decision to Explore Community Living

If you have decided to pursue senior community living options on behalf of your loved one, then we have a list of assumptions that run parallel to those made by individuals who have decided to age in place at home. Despite different outcomes, the paths to reach a decision are often the same. As always, the biggest assumption is that you're pursuing the wish of the aging senior in your life. You may not have perfect agreement from all parties involved that this is the best solution, but the decision has been reached that "home" no longer maximizes the rewards of safe, fulfilling daily living. You likely arrived at this spot through some messy discussions, but you can breathe once again and start to take actions that will help create a more fully functioning, richer life for your loved one than they have today.

Similar to the earlier discussion about aging at home, there is some jargon within senior community living that requires some simplification. All you need to understand is the basic terminology to be able to separate the chaff from the grain, and the fluff from what is real. For instance, when you hear in a community that they have a fabulous life enrichment director, you'll know they're talking about activities. You'll find that a lot of the confusion people experience when they tour senior communities comes about because of localized "spins" on old terms, plus some meaningful variations in structure that could make a real difference to you.

We'll look at each of the major types of senior living communities individually: independent living, assisted living, resident care homes, memory care, and continuing care retirement communities. After you've had a chance to narrow your focus based on your loved one's needs and the type of communities available in your area or your loved one's area, we'll look at the touring process, from the first visit at each community, to survival of the fittest among all properties you've seen, to an actual decision, and how to maximize time on move-in day. How to begin? If you're like me, searching the Internet comes high on the list. However, here's a caveat that needs to be explained.

When you begin searching online for senior-living options within a basic geography, you will immediately see a variety of long-term care placement services. They sound very appealing. Like any bit of advertising, they know the right words to use to snag your interest and perhaps even to play on your slightly conflicted state of mind. For instance, are you doing the right thing for your dad? Will he be happy living in an apartment instead of his house of thirty years? Will he make friends? Eat right? Think you've dumped him and run?

The placement services fully understand the situation you're in, and they also know the variety of options available within your geography. Plus, the ads say their services are free to you, so everything's good, right? The answer, unfortunately, is maybe or maybe not, depending on the totality of your circumstances.

There's actually quite a bit about placement services to like, and some of the agencies do a very good job of helping family members and seniors find a good "fit" for their needs. For the sake of full disclosure on this topic, know that as a community sales and marketing director, I have benefitted from potential "leads" that came directly from a placement service. Sometimes the "leads" called and toured my community, sometimes it was a good "fit," and they moved in. All too many times I never heard from the "leads," and the agency and I spent a lot of time trying but never reaching them through the phone number or email given.

The real point is not that agencies are used by individuals who want to get information but who have no intention of speaking with the advisors again, though that sometimes happens. The real point is that if you use a placement agency, they will provide you with a list of communities and their addresses that may fit your needs, some "insider" information, and a name of who to contact at the community. And if you find a community through them that will be your father's new "home," and if he signs a contract to move in and becomes a resident, it is true: the cost to you for the information rendered by the placement service is absolutely nothing out of pocket. It may, however, cost you in an entirely different way.

If one of the long-term care placement services sent me a lead that ended up moving into my community, then the agency had a contract with my community, and we paid for the leads that convert to actual move-ins. That's why it's free for you to use the service. The better the advisor knows my community, the more urging can be done on my behalf to get the family to my front door. The contracts vary slightly from community to community regarding the amount paid the agency, but compensation ranges from 70 percent to 100 percent of the first month's rent and care charges. Agencies also don't have contracts with all communities within any given market.

In combination, what this means to you is that the free services and referral list you get will consist of only the communities with whom the placement agency has a contract. If they've done a thorough job of wrapping up a large market with all communities contracted, then that's good news for you. But if they haven't done that, or if the advisor you talk to has a few favorite communities that always get the leads, or if it's been a slow month and the leads you receive (unbeknownst to you) happen to pay the most to the agency for a move-in, then that's not particularly good news. The true cost of the arrangement may be that you never get to hear about what might be the perfect community for your father because they haven't contracted with the placement agency. So, caveat emptor, buyer beware. Go in with eyes wide open, and have a list of deeply probing questions for the agency. The better you know what type of senior housing you're seeking and why, including your cost limitations, the more control you'll have.

As an alternative to senior placement agency, you might prefer the one on one, more personalized services of a case manager. Depending on the geography you've selected for your search, case managers have become fairly plentiful, and finding one should not be difficult. For instance, see either Case Management Society of America at http://www.cmsa.org or National Association of Professional Care Managers at http://member-find.caremanager.org. As always, you must do your homework: interview them, clarify costs, and seek past customers to gauge satisfaction levels.

I didn't personally use the services of a case manager when I was caring for my parents, but I've had several, always by themselves, call on me at the community level and found them to be smartly thorough in seeking relevant information for their client. The case managers I dealt with captured a complete but personalized picture of our community that included our mission, what we looked like, the expansiveness or limitations of our services, our flexibility or lack thereof, and a feel for our resident population. In essence, without ever sharing who their client was, they developed a clear snapshot of the community on which the client family and senior could decide to tour and investigate further, or not. If you prefer a personalized approach for sorting through community options, then a case manager's expertise could make them a viable partner as you limit communities to those fitting your circumstances.

For More Information

David Spiegel, "The Questionable Lure of Free Long-Term Care Placement Services," Kaiser Health News, July 28, 2011

http://www.kaiserhealthnews.org/Columns/2011/July/072811spiegel.aspx.

Michelle Singletary, "Due Diligence," Washington Post, Sept. 25, 2012

http://www.washingtonpost.com/business/due-diligence/2012/09/25/9ff4e8da-074e-11e2-a10c-fa5a255a9258_story.html.

Diane C. Lade, "Services Eager to Show Seniors the Way to a Home," Sun Sentinel, Nov.18, 2012

articles.sun-sentinel.com/2012-11-18/health/fl-senior-placement-businesses-20121117_1_seniors-care-facilities-franchises.

Case Management Society of America, accessed October 18, 2014

http://www.cmsa.org/Consumer/tabid/61/Default.aspx.

National Association of Professional Care Managers, accessed October 15, 2014

http://memberfinder.caremanager.org/.

CHAPTER EIGHTEEN

Independent Living

Independent-living facilities have changed over the years, due largely to the declines in our economy and, most especially, the bottom falling out of the housing market. Many seniors saw large losses in what was oftentimes their biggest and brightest investment—their homes. As real estate values plummeted during our most recent Recession, owners found the homes they had counted on to finance housing decisions during their years of declining health had become instead a (sometimes vastly) diminished asset. Was the perceived value of their homes too optimistic from the start? Perhaps, but many seniors nevertheless decided to stay in their homes instead of downsizing and wait for housing values to return to more respectable levels. They ultimately considered moving to senior living communities when a crisis demanded that they do so. The result changed the face of Independent Living.

During the intervening years while we've all waited for the economy to bounce back, time has brought countless changes to our lives. Younger generations may have enjoyed improved strong health, more rewarding work with an improved financial picture, or a growing circle of family and friends, but time is never kind to our seniors. They became frailer as the years passed, making the decision to postpone downsizing or moving into a choice with often dire consequences. For some seniors, declining health and the resulting effects were gradual; for others, a health crisis sharply curbed their abilities to care for themselves without assistance from others. Together as a group, however, the time to choose moving to an independent-living community has been replaced with the need to do so, and often, quickly. Gone are the days when everyone came to see what community living was about because they were planning for a time somewhere down the road. Curiosity and planning have largely been replaced by necessity.

These changes have resulted in an older, frailer group of residents in independent living, more walkers, and more wheelchairs. There are directors throughout the hierarchy of management in senior-living communities who claim that there is really no such thing as independent living anymore, that it's what assisted living used to be, and the folks who are now in assisted living are the residents who used to be in need of a nursing home. I hold fast to an unpopular position and completely disagree. It may take a firmer mindset than it once did because of the changed visual, and it definitely takes a variety of choices at every turn to service residents' needs—which is, to me, how a good community should operate anyway—but it certainly doesn't mean the more recent wave of residents makes the independent segment unworkable. Yes, it's different than it used to be, but if sufficient choices for residents are built into the framework of the community, it can be a long and happy chapter.

This dilemma came to me conversationally when I showed my community to some prospective residents and their families. If the prospective resident was fairly young, mobile, and very "with it" (according to family), they sometimes didn't appreciate the older, frailer look of the community's residents and couldn't see themselves fitting in with this group. I tried to explain that some of the folks they might have noticed had been with us for five or maybe even ten years, and that they have aged and even declined in health with us in their home. And, I would point out, we extend this same warmth and acceptance to all of our residents, whether they're the newly arrived or those who have been with us the longest. Conversely, some of our own residents—typically, but not always, the ones toward the younger end of the spectrum—would see me after touring a potential resident and ask me, "So, is that person I saw you with moving in?" After answering them as noncommittally as possible, the resident would continue, "We're just getting all the really old and sick people these days. Why can't we get some younger people who aren't so debilitated?" What I really wanted to say to everyone on both sides of the fence is that there but by the grace of God and Time we all go!

Given that independent living will differ slightly from community to community regarding their services, the following generalities are still true. Communities have a variety of rental apartment sizes (studio, one-bedroom, two-bedroom, and often some creations of their own in-between these sizes) that residents furnish with their own belongings. The apartments generally have a full kitchen, a bathroom with tub and shower, living room, one or more bedrooms, and ample closet space; sometimes they have a washer and dryer in the unit, but more likely there's a laundry center or two on each floor. Additional storage space and a parking space for a car are almost always assigned. Residents bring in furniture, linens, pictures for the walls, dishes, glasses, silverware, and all the tabletop knick-knacks that create a warm, home-like environment. Most communities have no problem if you want to paint the bedroom your mother's favorite color or paint accent walls in rooms to break up the generic eggshell-colored walls, but this will be an additional cost that you'll have to cover.

One of the biggest draws in senior community living is the dining room, because almost everyone likes the luxury of having meals cooked and served to their table every day. This doesn't mean, however, that everyone is always thrilled with the food. In my experience, comments about any given meal will be just about evenly split between pros and cons, and even the most popular meals—say, pot roast, meat loaf, or spaghetti—will still have its naysayers: It wasn't as good as Mom used to make. Some communities are even creating dining rooms that become a major selling point, using a combination of specially trained chefs, top-tier restaurant menus, or elegant ambiance. The meal plans will vary, but there will be a standard plan by which residents don't have to cook for themselves. One place I worked had three meals each day included with the rent. Another community had dinner every night with the choice of either breakfast or lunch included with rent. Another still had a heavy continental breakfast, no lunch, and dinner every night that was a part of the rental package.

Food service and the gaps in community meal plans tie in directly with transportation services, because there will be shopping needs to fill refrigerators and cupboards. Many residents in independent living still drive, though certainly not all of them, and the minibus transportation is important. You'll want to find out about the frequency and the routes, whether or not there are multiple stops (for example, a grocery store and a bank during the same outing), and how long they have to shop in the stores. This is the type of information you can get when you tour the communities. It's been my experience that it's perfectly okay for family members and friends to help with shopping and bring in the supplies weekly, especially if the resident doesn't want to ride the bus or can no longer drive where they want to go. There will also often be a little general store within the community where residents can purchase toiletries and snacks to get by until a planned shopping trip.

Independent-living communities will have on-site entertainment and activities. Families and seniors tend to either minimize the importance of activities altogether or expect more variety and better quality than can be found short of a cruise ship. From my experience, the important thing is this: you just never know how your loved one will react to the local offerings until they settle in, get comfortable, and decide for themselves. I've seen residents who said before moving into the community that activities and entertainment weren't important to them at all. They positioned themselves as readers and television watchers, but before long they used the community library or started reading and watching TV in the community gathering room. I've also seen ladies who initially scoffed at Bingo, but they became regulars who almost always told me how much money they won (a dollar or two) when they had a good day. It's all about socializing, being with people, getting out of the apartment, and finding others who want to do the same. My advice is to curtail expectations, don't nag and push, but wait and see. And the same applies to the entertainment provided. Sometimes it's very good, sometimes it's not so hot. But is gives them an experience to share and talk about later.

Independent living serves a specific segment of the senior population and is a good fit for potential residents who are squarely within its limits. Perhaps their current living situation has become too much for them to handle by themselves. Maybe grocery shopping and meal preparation have become difficult, and eating habits are changing as a result. Or maybe the declining number of personal relationships is creating signs of depression and withdrawal symptoms. A number of friends or family members passing away, plus neighbors moving out of the area, can make anyone struggle with loneliness. Perhaps some of these changes have been addressed in their current home by a number of individuals who help throughout the day, but typically there's something missing from the home environment that causes it to no longer work well. Even if the something is never fully identified, it's at this point that people start looking at community options.

In independent living, the building and landscape are maintained by the staff, housekeeping is provided, shopping and making meals is minimized, and the residents are surrounded by others with similar needs and interests. The daily demands of upkeep and maintenance become a worry of the past. If your loved one has developed relationships with people hired to help them at home, they can still help them in their community setting or visit as a guest (unless the relationships have been built around help with cleaning, cutting the grass and gardening, driving them for local shopping, or cooking dinner for them, then they've been replaced by staff positions).

Healthcare attention is the one area of services where independent living has limitations. Managers and staff will be present throughout the daytime hours, so someone is nearby if your loved one is sick or in need of emergency help. Keep in mind, however, that the department personnel—who are well trained in their positions, enjoy helping seniors, and in general have very big hearts—do not have medical training. During nighttime hours, staff count drops dramatically and it's a different story altogether. Many independent-living communities only have security guards on throughout the night, and it's often one person to answer the phone and take messages while the other one walks the building and checks exits; then they alternate jobs to stay fresh during the night. Perhaps the best answer to nighttime staffing has already been described in Leigh and Uncle Robert's tale in chapter 3. Robert's facility, part of a very large nationwide chain of independent-living communities, answers this issue by requiring that their two manager couples live on site and rotate for night duty. As you remember, however, even this has its limitations: they are there to answer calls for help, but without medical training, their options are limited to calling 911.

As the population attracted to independent living has changed, the communities have tried to make additions and changes to keep up with evolving interests. The entering seniors may be older than the group was five or ten years ago, but they're an informed group who tend to be interested in taking care of themselves at the urging of their proactive doctors. At the community level, this has translated into seniors and family members asking about whether there are doctors and nurses present, either on staff or visiting regularly, and what exercise options are available.

The resulting wellness center has been a boon to independent living. Usually staffed by an outside healthcare agency, a wellness center often hosts a cheery, welcoming staff that helps residents look forward to checking in regularly for blood pressure tests, weigh-ins, and just to chat. The space is also used for doctor visits, with the appointment schedule handled by the wellness staff. "Wellness" becomes a topic of interest and pride in the community, with the agency staff using their ideas and contacts to provide guest speakers who offer small seminars on a variety of topics in the community. In addition to the wellness centers, communities are also likely to offer an exercise room, some with individualized fitness programs tailored for the new residents.

Depending on the current needs of your loved one, there could well come a day—sooner or later—when the independent model no longer works to cover your loved one's needs. At that point you can inquire about adding a caregiver in the apartment for one-on-one assurances throughout the night, but the response may be that the resident no longer fits the independent model. If you happen to be involved with a community that has more flexibility, and they do exist, then you can add your own personnel to create the peace of mind you need . . . and the oversight for safety's sake your loved one may need.

The very best situation I know is a community where I worked that was independent living on three floors and assisted living on one floor, but it was the flexibility and emphasis on resident and family choice that made it so successful. If, for example, an independent resident wanted a nighttime caregiver instead of relocating to assisted living on another floor where medical staff was on all night, then the resident's choice was fully supported. Or, the part-time caregiver could turn into a full-time caregiver as needs change, or hospice could be added. The point was always that the community was the residents' home, and it was our job to get them what they needed and wanted to make their home work for them.

If you are looking at independent-living communities, my hope for you is that you find this type of commitment and flexibility for your loved one. It certainly served my mother well. When she passed away from heart failure at ninety-six years old, she was still living in her apartment in the aforementioned community, still thinking of herself as "independent," still using her rollator-walker with a seat to go to meals twice a day and attend activities and entertainment of her choosing. Was she old and weak? Yes, she was, but she was tough, had a good sense of humor, loved her family, and she thought she was in charge. That's what mattered to me.

CHAPTER NINETEEN

Assisted Living

An assisted-living community has all of the services and amenities described in the last chapter on independent living, but there is a central difference: independent living's limiting factor of not having nursing assistance available at the community around the clock is the core feature of assisted living. As seniors age and decline in their abilities to care for themselves the way they wish they could, evening and nighttime hours become problematic. Crises often occur when no one is around to help. However, for the assisted-living communities, those same hours are just another shift to fully staff with skilled caregivers.

Assisted living is all about caring for residents who can no longer live alone, providing assistance, and being present to provide scheduled and unscheduled help. You'll find the nightshift reduced in staff count, but the key element is that a registered nurse or other licensed healthcare professional will be present at all times. The R.N. is there to supervise the staff and care of the residents, interface with doctors, pharmacists, and medical facilities, answer resident and family questions or concerns, provide injections, and handle medication management for all residents. On occasion, there will be communities that provide a nurse on-call during the midnight shift or share an R.N. with another building on their campus. This was the situation at two communities where I worked. The on-call nurse regularly receives nighttime calls (and sometimes must return to the building) while the shared R.N. does lots of running between buildings. Though the differences between assisted and independent living may center on resident healthcare services, it extends from there into an entirely different product than independent living.

Initially conceived as a residential alternative to nursing homes, the assisted-living concept is only twenty to twenty-five years old but has grown into a full-fledged industry. There are more than 31,000 communities nationwide with over one million residents. Assisted living's mission is to provide the needed assistance so seniors can live as independently as possible within a community setting. This intermediate level of long-term care provides assistance with activities of daily living (bathing, dressing, toileting, walking, eating, and medication management) so that the resident can otherwise live independently. Assisted living is less expensive (2014 national median monthly rate is $3,500 or $42,000 per year) than a private nursing home room (2014 national median monthly rate is $7,300 or $87,600 per year). Assisted-living communities—all without the nursing home's twenty-four-hour skilled nursing feature and its higher level of supervision/care—is a much less restrictive environment.

Before a potential resident makes a final decision and contracts to join an assisted-living community, the local director of nursing completes a nursing assessment of the senior interested in receiving services. Should the potential resident ultimately move into the community, the assessment will become the resident's Plan of Care. Together with the resident and family representative or friend, they will discuss the tasks throughout the day that would be easier/safer with assistance (bathing, dressing, toileting, walking, eating, medication management), the frequency of help needed (daily, multiple times a day, weekly), and who will be helping (resident aide, nursing assistant, nurse). From the assessment and development of a care plan, two questions can be answered. First, whether or not the potential resident's needs are within the scope of services the community can provide, and second, how much the services will cost.

The monthly cost of assisted living is presented in a variety of ways, which makes it a little confusing to compare costs from location to location, but basically there are two components: rent and personal care services, which will be the assistance performed by the nursing staff. Rent will generally include the apartment, meals, housekeeping, maintenance, security, transportation, and various other amenities, such as access to exercise, health and wellness programs, social and recreational activities, and personal laundry services. The cost of personal care services, the "assistance" part of assisted living provided by the nursing staff, might be presented in any number of ways and will vary by community. Some of the more common ones you may find include all inclusive (one rate, no matter how much help is needed), ala carte (itemized, pay for service), and tiered (bundled groups of services with increasing costs for each group).

There are advantages and disadvantages to each method, which may be more or less important to you and your situation as you think them through. The all-inclusive plan is great for budgeting purposes because you know the cost will be the same each month. It's also a particularly good value for residents on the high end of the service scale. Even though it may not seem like a particularly a good deal for a resident who only needs a little help, you nevertheless have the peace of mind that as needs increase, the monthly charge will not. Pay for service is straightforward, but the bill is never the same from month to month. If, for example, your mother catches the flu bug and needs a lot of help getting through the days of feeling rotten, the bill will reflect the additional man hours and may be a big surprise. Tiered services can be easy to understand but rigid; take a serious look at what services are in each tier. If a service is newly needed that's not in your current tier, the price jumps to the cost of the higher tier. Conversely, new residents can come in at a higher tier than they may need after health concerns stabilize from the good care they receive; the tier will reduce and so will the price (after the director of nursing re-evaluates and paperwork is signed).

All of this will seem more relevant to you when you have narrowed the communities to a choice of one or two and you're putting together all of the detailed information. Cost is a big factor, however, and how the price is determined will ultimately matter a lot to you. Most locations will bill month to month, although you might occasionally find a community that requires a long-term arrangement of a year or more. When you add the rent portion of the bill together with the care portion, you're talking about a significant financial decision, especially when the cost is extrapolated over the many years we all hope our loved ones continue living.

More than forty states have a version of assisted-living communities funded under the banner "Home and Community Based Waiver Program" (HCBS), which makes the assisted living concept available to low-income seniors. Medicaid HCBS, authorized under Section 1915(i) of the Social Security Act, was designed to help states provide Medicaid beneficiaries with the ability to reach numerous service options—either to continue living in their homes or to explore assisted community living—as an alternative to long-term nursing home placement. If this proposition interests you, and especially if your loved one has very limited resources and is teetering on the edge of qualifying for Medicaid services, there are many states that have strong affordable senior-living programs, generally known as Supportive Living Facilities (SLFs). They create viable options for many seniors who can't afford to pay privately for the cost of regular assisted-living communities. And it may well be worth your time to investigate.

State regulations govern assisted-living communities in all fifty states, and each community operates under its own state license that must be displayed in an easily visible location within the community. Although the administrative agency's title will vary from state to state, the oversight and resulting uniformity is virtually the same. The state regulatory agency inspects each community yearly to make certain it is following the rules and regulations set forth to maintain its license to operate. Each deficiency or violation of the administrative code found during the examination will be documented and resolved in a timely manner to the satisfaction of the state examiner and the governing body they represent. The remedies and sanctions for deficiencies range from formal warnings with immediate correction to fines that range from $500 up to $10,000 or more for each infraction. Covering multiple days of examination in each community, the state's inspection is a very exacting process designed to maintain the highest levels of care for each and every resident receiving services from assisted-living's nursing staff.

You are the beneficiary of the state survey. First, you know there is a governing body with a very watchful eye on the professionals and services designed to provide the care your loved one needs and is paying considerable sums of money to receive. Second, as a practical matter, every community has a serious business need to protect their operating license by making sure all services contracted are performed as promised and are squarely within the mandates of their governing state code.

Their business depends on employees doing their job well and making you and yours happy. While I'm not advocating ripping a community's assisted-living license off the wall and waving it around every time there's an issue regarding care that concerns you, I do believe a little knowledge that's based in reality can strengthen your side of the conversation.

Lastly, when you're done exploring options and have narrowed your choices to one or two assisted-living communities, you have the ability to see for yourself how the community performed on their most recent state survey. This can be accomplished by either asking at the community level to see a copy of their last state survey or, if you prefer more anonymity, requesting the report in writing from the state regulatory agency in charge.

Since the agency in charge of regulating assisted-living communities varies from state, I have used examples from Illinois. With the notations provided, you will be able to use the citations as an example to find the relevant information for the state where you're searching.

For More Information

Pat Moran, "Assisted Living Intimidation," Senior Housing Forum, October 24, 1914

http://www.seniorhousingforum.net/blog/2014/10/26/assisted-living-intimidation.

Kim Severson, "Grandma's Meatloaf? Hardly. Her Retirement Home Now Has a 3-Star Chef," New York Times, Dining and Wine, September 7, 2014

http://www.nytimes.com/2014/09/08/dining/grandmas-meat-loaf-hardly-her-retirement-home-now-has-a-3-star-chef.html.

"Assisted Living Information," American Federation of America, accessed November 7, 2014

http://www.alfa.org/alfa/Assisted_Living_Information.asp

"State Regulations and Licensing Information," Assisted Living Federation of America, accessed November 7, 2014 http://www.alfa.org/alfa/State_Regulations_and_Licensing_Informat.asp.

"National Overview of 1915I HCBS Waivers," Centers for Medicare & Medicaid Services, last modified Sept. 9, 2013, accessed November 11, 2014

www.cms.gov/Outreach-and-Education/American-Indian-Alaska-Native/AIAN/LTSS-Roadmap/Resources/State-Federal-Relationships/National-Overview-of-1915c-HCBS-Waivers.html.

"Home and Community-Based Services in Assisted Living Facilities," Department of Health and Human Services, Office of Inspector General, accessed Nov. 11, 2014

http://www.oig.hhs.gov/oei/reports/oei-09-08-00360.pdf.

"Home and Community Based Services Waiver Program: Elderly," accessed Nov. 11, 2014

http://www2.illinois.gov/hfs/MedicalPrograms/HCBS/Pages/elderly.aspx.

Title 77 of the Illinois Administrative Code: Public Health, Chapter I. Department of Public Health, subchapter c. Long-Term Care Facilities, Part 295: Assisted Living and Shared Housing Establishment Code, accessed Nov. 14, 2014

http://ilga.gov/commission/jcar/admincode/077/07700295sections.html.

Section 295.1030 Information to Be Made Available to the Public by the Department, Illinois Administrative Code, accessed Nov. 14, 2014

http://ilga.gov/commission/jcar/admincode/077/07700295sections.html.

CHAPTER TWENTY

Resident Care Homes

Resident care homes are located in traditional houses in residential neighborhoods and, as a result, are difficult to pigeonhole by consistent characteristics. No two resident care homes are exactly alike in design, services, personnel, cost parameters, entrance qualifications, and depending on where you're searching, whether there is a state licensing requirement concerning levels of care and services provided. Complicating it further, residential care homes are also known as board and care homes, personal care homes, and adult family care homes, all with small but potentially important differences between them. This means that if resident care homes become a top choice to fulfill your needs, you will need to be extra thorough investigating your top choices.

In the terms we've been using, resident care homes most resemble assisted living in the care that can be provided for the residents, but the total number of residents is tiny in comparison. Whereas true assisted living generally means a corporately owned building of rentable private apartments, care homes are privately owned residential houses that have become a business. The exact number of residents residing in each home will vary depending on the size of the house, but, unlike assisted living, you are more likely to find shared bedrooms mixed in with private ones—some sharing bathrooms, some not. Additionally, you'll find living rooms, kitchens, dining rooms, and possible porches or patios functioning as common space to be shared by the residents. In every situation, you'll find a supervised, small group environment with personalized care services designed to meet a variety of individual needs. Like assisted-living communities, resident care homes are designed for the seniors who can no longer live well and safely by themselves but who do not need twenty-four-hour nursing care.

Resident care homes can be found nationwide, but the number of homes from state to state varies widely. Unlike assisted living, which is state regulated but with no federal standards, care homes may or may not have state licensing requirements about levels of care, services, and staff. California has the greatest number of resident care homes, called Resident Care Facilities for the Elderly (RCFE), and the tightest licensing requirements: each home operates under the state standards mandated by the California Department of Social Services, Community Care License Division. On-site inspections occur every five years, with non-compliant homes inspected annually. This rulemaking and enforcement create uniformity within the California offerings and, for our purposes, make their resident care homes easier to use as the benchmark for a product that might work for you. Clearly, all readers won't be looking in California, but it provides a starting point from which you can compare.

California Resident Care Homes position themselves as having six to fifteen beds; that definition puts them between assisted living with sixteen-plus beds and board and care homes with four to six beds. Locally owned with shared rooms, RCFEs offer room, board, housekeeping, supervision, and personal care assistance with hygiene, dressing, transferring, eating, and walking. Medication can be stored and distributed, but the resident must be able to self-administer. There are limiting factors: no tube feedings, no treatment of open bedsores, and nothing that requires twenty-four-hour nursing care such as IV treatments. As non-medical facilities, RCFEs aren't required to have registered nurses and certified nursing assistants on staff, though most do on a shift basis. It's possible that the supervisor who lives at the community could be a licensed R.N., but there is no requirement.

Costs in California RCFEs vary significantly, which is the same in other states. The low end of cost, $1,000 per month in California, reflects those residents living on Supplemental Security Income (SSI) or Medicaid equivalent, though there are fewer and fewer beds state-wide available for this segment of the population. Like most states, they want you to pay privately for a year or two before converting to low-income rates, if and when there are beds available. The high end of the RCFEs reaches $9,000 per month, driven by the higher cost of dementia and hospice care that require more one-on-one supervision. The 2014 median RCFE cost is $3,750 per month, with higher or lower costs driven by the individual care that's needed. Long-term care insurance and veterans' benefits may offset monthly costs.

Each resident care facility in California is required to show you its most recent state inspection if you ask to see it, which would probably be the easiest and most timely way to view results. The Department of Social Services maintains only minimal online information. The only other way to see a copy of a facility's latest inspection is to request the public record for that facility at the district office of the Community Care License Division.

Generally speaking, these characteristics—based on the uniformity derived from California's Resident Care Facilities –—apply to other states' Resident Care Homes.

There may or may not be state licensing requirements

Bedrooms are private or shared

Standard services: supervision, meals, snacks, limited activities or entertainment

Custodial care: laundry, housekeeping, transportation to doctor

Varying levels of assistance (all non-medical) and likely incremental cost: toileting, bathing, dressing, transferring, eating, walking

Medication reminders or administration

Generally nursing oversight but not at all times

Staff can range from R.N. to recent immigrants; homeowner could live-in; shifts of caregivers likely (inquire about background checks.)

Limitations: no tube feedings, no treatment for open bedsores, no requirements for twenty-four-hour nursing. Some allow hospice (this is by license waiver), some are adaptable to non-ambulatory needs (if applicable, check each facility to be certain)

Cost ranges from a low of $1,500 per month to an average of $3,500–$4,500. The high end averages $5,000–$6,000 per month for facilities specializing in dementia care. Some homes do not accept Medicaid, and most that do accept it will want one to two years private pay before converting to Medicaid. Long-term care insurance and veterans' benefits, if available to the resident, generally apply.

My one personal experience with resident care homes was at arm's length but extremely positive. A close friend of mine placed her mother, Eileen, in a California resident care facility, and despite Eileen's increasing dementia, she resided there safely and happily for years. The family was extremely satisfied with the care and attention she received, but their point of departure was necessitated by something you should keep in mind: with late stage Alzheimer's—and certainly with other disease processes as well—nursing needs will likely become more than resident care homes can handle. You will be moving again at some point in time. My work-related experience was more direct. I lost several potential new residents to less expensive resident care homes that would allow transitioning to Medicaid when personal funds were depleted. That is an important piece of the puzzle I could never offer.

Like any of the other options in senior community living, the "fit" has to be a good one between the home and your loved one. We go all the way back to the question in chapter 1: Who Is This Person? You have to know exactly what would work and what won't. I've seen seniors who are overwhelmed by the appearance of assisted-living communities that they feel are too big or too fancy; maybe a residential care home would work for a person who feels that way. Or perhaps an assisted-living community seems like it has too many residents and too many staff members "always on the go" caring for residents; maybe a smaller home-like setting would work better and seem less hectic for that person. You'll be the one to decide if resident care homes are a viable option for your situation, but if you go in that direction, plan to visit often and dig deep with your questions. Be certain to ask about their license (check through your state Department of Aging). What health crises or conditions could make remaining there impossible? Which family members of past or current residents would be open to speaking with you by phone about the home and its care?

In spite of wanting to help seniors and their family members find the type of community environment they wanted and needed (while hoping that it might be my community), I always believed that the right residence had to be the "right fit" and the "right time." There is, in my opinion, no one size fits all—or, more especially, no one community that is the right community for everybody. It just doesn't work like that. The community has to feel right, as determined by who that senior is at their core. So if your loved one might do better in a very small community of seniors who reside together in an actual house with supervised living and help with personal care, then by all means investigate the option of resident care homes. You'll find the best operators talk to you in terms of how they promote a healthy lifestyle for their residents with a wide range of "community" and social opportunities, how they offer socialization and a high quality of life in addition to caring for their basic health care needs with services. Trust yourself: you'll know it's the "right fit" at the "right time" when you experience it, and it will feel right.

For More Information

Resident Care Facilities for the Elderly, California Advocates for Nursing Home Reform (CANHR), accessed Oct. 30, 2014

http://www.canhr.org/RCFE/rcfe_what.htm.

Resident Care Homes, A Place for Mom, accessed Nov. 15, 2014

http://www.aplaceformom.com/care-homes#cost.

Residential Care Homes, SeniorHomes.com, accessed Nov. 15, 2014

http://www.seniorhomes.com/p/care-homes/

http://www.idph.il.us/pdf/Life_Care_Update.pdf

Pat Moran, Assisted Living Intimidation, Senior Housing Forum, October 24, 1914

http://www.seniorhousingforum.net/blog/2014/10/26/assisted-living-intimidation.

CHAPTER TWENTY-ONE

Memory Care

Those of you reading this chapter most carefully have an additional serving of heartbreak and stress on your plate, and without knowing any of you individually, I offer you empathy, encouragement, and most especially more strength than you know you have to get through the days. As you become more and more wrapped up in caregiving obligations, you see the person you knew and loved fade before your very eyes. As you well know by now, there are good days and bad, ups and downs that seem to play out in a pattern of their own, making each day, each encounter with your loved one difficult to predict. You've probably learned by now to accept the irregularity of the pattern, and that's a good thing. Try as hard as you can to enjoy the good days, capture the moments to hold close to your soul at some later time, and then move on as best you can. Become available in response to the day at hand. Try to let go of what once was and meet them where they are that day . . . no matter where that is.

This is not going to be a chapter on the disease process of memory loss, Alzheimer's, or any of the identifiable types of dementia; you need other authors for that, which you'll easily find in print or online. What I can offer instead is a narrow but important piece of the puzzle to help you discover the best memory care community environment to meet your needs today and, hopefully, through end of life. You want one permanent move, not several moves trying to get it right, because the confusion brought on by massive change is frightening to those with serious memory loss. You cannot help them understand the change from home to home. No matter how carefully and logically you explain why the move is necessary, no matter how much they seem to understand at the time, they will forget the reason why they are suddenly in a strange place with strange people. This chapter will help you look for choices, seek answers, and make decisions to get it right the first time. Can their confusion be completely eliminated as you move them from wherever they live now to the selected memory care community? Probably not. But depending on where they are in their memory decline, the confusion can be minimized and become significantly less traumatic when you've discovered the right community with the right trained caregivers.

In preparation for your search, there are steps you can take that will prepare you for traveling through community options, meeting nursing staff, and assessing the possibilities of what's available to meet your needs. The first thing you need to do, if it hasn't been done already, is have a medical assessment completed by a doctor to provide a formal diagnosis. The usual path is through your loved one's general practitioner, who will make the referral to a neurologist, neuropsychologist, or geriatrician for the actual assessment. The diagnosis will be required as a preliminary step for entrance into a memory care facility. The precaution is simply so they know—and you know—that the right combination of people, needs, and services are likely to produce successful outcomes. You can go so far as to tour communities, make a selection, sign the contract, and even move belongings into their future room, but individuals will not be moved into residency without the formal diagnosis completed.

Consider making a list to jog your memory regarding your loved one's behavioral changes. Think in terms of chapter 1, Who Is This Person? You're searching for a combination of broad brush strokes and intimate details illustrating who they were and how they navigated through life before their days were overcome with new behaviors brought on by the disease itself. Who were they, and what did they do for both work and pleasure? When you begin touring individual memory care communities, this will help you look for specific programming and evidence of how individual care needs are met throughout the day. Even before that, it will help in conversations about possible facilities as you talk with friends, associates, neighbors, or anyone you feel has had exposure to some of the same situations you're experiencing. And it will help prepare you for questions asked during the doctor's assessment.

The trick will be to concentrate on creating the list, all the while consciously choosing not to think about memories associated with the past. As best you can, think of it only as a mechanical production of information, something that will lead to a more efficient outcome rather than a memoir of sorts. Like others in your situation, you'll find that the more productive and efficient you can be during these stressful times, the more easily you will get through the day. And when you actually begin talking with a doctor or touring memory care communities, no matter how emotional the time becomes, your list is complete. You won't have to produce details while your focus is on evaluating the surroundings or worry later that you forgot something important.

New residents and memory care personnel alike can make tremendous use of these lists. The opportunity to freely perform familiar tasks helps calm and comfort the residents and encourages feelings of productivity. I remember many meetings in a memory care manager's office when one of our residents strolled in, smiled, and started straightening up papers on the manager's desk. She had worked for years as an administrative assistant and she never left without putting the pens, pencils, and paper clips neatly in their proper place. We never let her leave without saying "nice job" and thanking her for her work. Another resident with a similar work history did a lot of filing, so she had a roll-top desk in one of the halls with colored files to sort and file. Often a manager would hand the resident an assortment of files and used printer paper while guiding her to her desk; later, there would be evidence that she had imposed order . . . perhaps meaningful only to her, but the desk was never a mess. There were residents who tended to baby dolls—washed, dressed, fed, and rocked them; women who "shopped" at the boutique; men who sorted fishing lures and fit together pieces of PVC pipe; others who dug in the dirt, their faces to the sun, planting plants when the weather was accommodating. The point is, these links to the residents' past came from family members' lists, connections to who the residents were and who they are still.

As you begin to decide which properties you want to visit, ones you may have heard about from your network of contacts or may have seen in print or online advertising, look at what the properties say they have to offer. Look closely at the details regarding activities throughout the day, dining services, staffing ratios, and security. If you find it vague, then make notes to yourself with specific questions. You'll likely find promises about keeping the residents meaningfully engaged throughout the day. How do they do that? What kind of activities are offered and how often? What's the staffing ratio to accomplish that? Look for an indication of resident choices that can be made at every turn, especially in activities and in the dining room. And how does meal service operate? The ideal dining experience includes making menu decisions like this: staff brings pre-arranged plates with meal choices to the tables for the residents to see and then choose between, which creates a less frustrating time for residents struggling with memory loss and unreliable vocabulary recall.

If your loved one has started to wander (you may hear it referred to as "exit seeking"), then you'll want to hear and see how the property handles risk of elopement. This is an enormous area of concern and often drives the decision to make the move to a secured (locked) community. But if every memory care community offers a secured environment, then the question still remains: How do they do it? What is their plan, by the minute (immediately at the minute the disappearance is known, at ten minutes following, then at twenty minutes, and at thirty minutes)? When you finally visit communities and talk to people working there, be prepared to ask, "What do you do when a resident is missing? How is the staff trained for elopement issues and how often? How many elopements have there been in the last several years, and what were the results?" You'll get the official answers from the resident care director, who is in charge of the memory care residence, but elopement questions are excellent choices to ask of individual staff members as well, away from the director.

Asking about personal care needs and how they're handled is pretty straightforward as regards current needs, but what you really want to know is this: what increased needs could prohibit your loved one from continuing to reside in this community through end of life? Press to discover the specific medical needs the community cannot meet by their license.

Do they allow hospice services?

Are doctors, nurses, and therapists of your choosing allowed to call on, examine, and treat your loved one? What are the rules and limitations of those visits?

Is transportation provided by the community to doctor visits?

Which staff member accompanies the resident to the doctor, and will the staff member take notes and report back to family?

On a daily basis, how often will your loved one get one-on-one personal help with hygiene, toileting, dressing, transferring, walking, or whatever other needs arise?

What's the ratio of staff to individual resident on each shift?

How is the personal care staff trained in memory care issues?

What is the mix of licensed/certified staff and non-licensed/certified staff?

What hours is an R.N. present in the community?

Even though the needs of memory care residents are much more complex than those of assisted-living residents, the vast majority of memory care residences operate under assisted-living licensure. As such, they will be inspected by the state on a regular basis, and the resulting evaluation will be available for you to read either at the local community level or through the state regulatory channels. Plan to ask to see the latest state assessment results. Also, decide who you want to ask to speak with regarding care provided to the residents at this community (current or past family members, satisfied customers, or someone who had specific challenges with the care).

When you finally tour memory care communities, don't be reluctant to take the time you need to feel comfortable, to look thoroughly at the community inside and out, and to ask all of your questions. You'll be meeting some of the managers and front-line staff as you tour, individuals who may be responsible for the love and care of someone dear to you, so I know you'll be prepared and ready to get the full picture. Similarly, if there's a department head that is not there but you want to talk with them specifically, don't hesitate to ask about a later appointment with them—it happens all the time. Above all, don't let them rush you, and don't be pushed into making a decision before you feel really ready. Their urgency is about their needs, not yours, so stand your ground until you've firmly decided you found the best solution.

For More Information

"Dementia Diagnosis and Diagnostic Testing," Alzheimer's Association, accessed November 23, 2014

http://www.alz.org/health-care-professionals/dementia-diagnosis-diagnostic-tests.asp#diff.

Rich Malley, "How to Find the Right Alzheimer's/Memory Care Community," SeniorAdvisor Blog, July 2014, accessed September 14, 2014

https://www.senioradvisor.com/blog/2014/07/how-to-find-alzheimers-memory-care/.

Debbie Howard, "Top 4 'Must Haves' Memory Care Benefits," Senior Living Smart, September 14, 2014

http://www.seniorlivingsmart.com/top-4-must-haves-memory-care-benefits/.

Andrea Catizone, "5 Outcomes of a Quality Dementia Care Program," Senior Living Smart, February 24, 2014, accessed September 14, 2015

http://www.seniorlivingsmart.com/5-outcomes-quality-dementia-care-program/.

Andrea Catizone, "The 3 P's of Reducing Elopement Risk (Prevention, Preparation, Performance)," Senior Living Smart, March and April, 2014, accessed September 14, 2014

http://www.seniorlivingsmart.com/3-ps-elopement-risk-management/.

https://www.alzheimersspeaks.com

CHAPTER TWENTY-TWO

Continuing Care Retirement Communities

So far we've discussed independent living, assisted living, resident care homes, and memory care communities as options for senior community living. Continuing Care Retirement Communities (CCRCs or Continuing Care Communities, also known as Life Care Communities) consist of independent, assisted, and memory care options, plus nursing home care, congregated on one piece of property and operating under single ownership. Sometimes the campus consists of one large building containing the various levels of care for the residents. Newer construction has more of a true campus look and feel with multiple buildings on several acres of land. CCRCs provide all of the services and care previously described in traditional retirement communities, but due to the wider range of ages, interests, and abilities of the residents, there is also more flexibility and a greater variety of amenities. Common offerings can include putting greens, spas, swimming pools, sport courts, and numerous on-site conveniences such as banks, gift shops, ice cream and coffee parlors, hair salons, and multiple dining venues.

Perhaps the greatest selling advantage enjoyed by CCRCs is their message that this is the resident's last move, that any lifestyle—regardless of the level of care required—is within their range of on-campus accommodations. By its very name, continuing care connotes the ability to "age in place," and CCRs routinely promise that a move away from its location will not be required for healthcare needs requiring a higher level of care than is covered by their licensure. With independent and assisted living, memory care, and skilled nursing, CCRCs do indeed have all of the bases covered. They're offering security and insurance that the care that's needed will be available on-site, in spite of whatever health declines may occur over the years. They also make the assurance that if you outlive your money, the community will cover all necessary expenses (if you have selected the appropriate contract). This can sound extremely attractive to a large variety of potential residents, perhaps none more so than couples. If spouses need different levels of care and must be separated, they nevertheless are still in close proximity to each other. In fact, this sounds so good that it begs the question: with advantages like these, why doesn't every senior move into a CCRC?

The answer to that question is both simple and, at the same time, the most complex part of choosing a CCRC. The most expensive of long-term care options, continuing care communities require a significant financial commitment that is well beyond the economic means of many seniors. Traditional retirement communities charge monthly rates without a long-term lease; CCRCs, on the other hand, require an initial "buy-in" fee in addition to monthly assessments (the equivalent of rent and services in a traditional retirement community). Given that every dollar estimate depends on variables such as the size and location of the unit chosen, the number of occupants, and the costs for level(s) of care, it's still possible to make some generalizations about financial outlay.

Entrance fees range from nearly $100,000 to $1 million or more. Functionally and in the aggregate, buy-in fees cover prepayment for care and provide coverage for the community's operational expenses. In "CCRC-language," the entrance fees are considered to be "refundable," in that 70 percent to 90 percent of the deposits revert to the residents' estate upon their death (or the death of the last remaining spouse). Additionally, monthly fees can range from $3,000 to $5,000 or more depending on a variety of factors. In many locations, there is an inverse correlation between the size of entrance fees and ongoing monthly assessments. Communities with higher upfront fees usually have lower monthly assessments, but those with lower entrance fees appear to make up the difference by charging higher monthly fees.

Given that individual CCRCs have the latitude to set their own pricing structure, as long as they remain within their corresponding state act and governing code, it's somewhat difficult to talk in detailed terms about costs. Details depend entirely on the specifics of the community and the choices made by the potential resident. One factor heavily influencing cost calculations: every incoming resident must choose between three different contracts that will govern their community stay with varying effects.

Life Care or Extended Contract (also known as Type-A contract): This is the most expensive option but offers unlimited, lifetime access to care (medical, assisted living, and skilled nursing) without an increase to the monthly fee.

Modified Contract: This option offers a set of services for a set amount of time, after which more services can be obtained but at higher monthly charges. If additional services are required before the lapse of time originally set, a daily rate may be charged.

Fee-for-Service Contract (also known as rental contracts): This option provides a lower monthly fee for independent living; however, assisted living and skilled nursing expenses are paid for at the daily market rate.

The impact of contract choice will make a tremendous difference financially and, at the same time, negatively impact predictability regarding cost projections. Without the benefit of the crystal ball we all wish we had, it's impossible to know what the future will bring in terms of needs and resulting costs as years pass. It may feel as though you're using "best guess" and "worst case" scenarios, but long-term financial health is one topic that must be exhausted. Not only is there the initial decision-making and its cost ramifications, but there may be charges above and beyond the entrance fee and monthly charges that need to be addressed.

Because of the long-term commitment built in to choosing a continuing care community and because of the difficulty pinning down cost specifics, there are several steps necessary to minimize surprises. If your loved one is seriously attracted to this particular solution, consider it a complex investment worthy of your time and effort to investigate. Be present to see and hear everything, and plan to take a copy of the contract to an elder law attorney prior to signing; be certain all fine print is thoroughly understood by everyone. It's all going to matter at some point on some unforeseeable day in the future. They will eventually need a higher level of care, so specifically what will that mean? If you're helping a couple plan for the future, one of them will need more care or will pass away before the other so, in detail, how will that be handled? What will that mean financially? Equally important, be certain that you understand the nuances of a percentage of the entrance fee going to their estate. Ask how the percentage will be determined. What are reasonable expectations on the timing of the return? Be certain you understand whether or not the release of funds is contingent upon the sale/lease of other similar/identical units that are "brand new" rather than your recently vacated and renovated unit, a process that has been known to delay results and unravel predictability.

In addition to the investment benefit of buying into a CCRC, there are some simple ways to double-check your potential buyer's enthusiasm about their decision. Before they sign on the dotted line, encourage them to request a "trial" weekend or, even better, a weeklong stay at the community to test the staying power of their choice. It's not an unusual request at all. Even with the traditional senior-living communities built on month-to-month leases with no investment ramifications beyond the timing of a thirty-day move-out notice, potential residents sometimes request a short trial period to test the waters before committing to a lease.

You'll probably find the CCRC in question has several guest suites for this purpose and, as a relatively inexpensive marketing tool, they will offer the stay as a complimentary service. Even if they don't offer to cover the costs, it's a minor investment to determine whether the community is really as perfect as it seems to be. Time spent on the campus would also provide an excellent opportunity for your loved one(s) to meet and talk with some of the residents. CCRCs tend to have active and involved residents, perhaps none more so than those who are engaged with the resident council, and the community positives and negatives would surely surface.

Whether or not the trial stay at the community actually takes place, try to find a way to encourage creating some quiet space and time to think (and talk) through a few of the most attractive promises. For instance, many retirees feel the CCRC concept and its benefits allow their children a way out, a means of not being "burdened" with their care during times of crisis and declining health. Granted, it appears that facilities are in place on campus to cover a multitude of potential health threats and the resulting changes in lifestyles, but many family members will still choose involvement in care and the advocacy that's often required. They'll want to be there. Can that emotional commitment really be changed by the location of buildings and services within a central campus? Our loved ones, and most especially our parents, often want to spare us from what they feel is the added responsibility of taking care of them during times of poor health, but a crisis is when relationships can show their strengths instead of deficits. Most people want the chance to help, and enjoying residency in a well-designed campus environment probably won't change that.

Perhaps you'll also want to carve out quiet space and time to think (and talk) through likely future-based scenarios, such as health events that demand different services than those currently needed. Even though higher-care needs are met within the CCRC community, it can often require a physical move to meet the different level of care. For example, in the aftermath of a severe stroke requiring skilled nursing and therapy services for an indefinite period of time to restore strength and physical skills, there is no alternative available to the resident except to be physically relocated to the skilled nursing unit. That may mean a different building, a different floor, or a specific wing of a building, but it is almost certainly a move from a less restrictive environment to the most restrictive environment. And it's a move: you can expect signs of Relocation Stress Syndrome.

If the patient happens to be one half of a couple residing in the CCRC, the healthy spouse may indeed be closer to the afflicted spouse than in other senior communities where the patient is temporarily moved across town to a hospital's skilled care wing or an unknown nursing home; however, there's still distinct separateness that looks and feels the same no matter where it takes place. Perhaps they will ultimately decide a CCRC's short drive, ride, or walk is better than a much longer one that makes them more dependent on coordinating help within their support system, and that's fine. At least they've thought through it and placed a value on what change will look and feel like when it becomes their reality.

As you know by now, senior-living communities are not federally regulated, and Continuing Care Retirement Communities are no different. Though CCRCs may be known by any of their various monikers, they are all regulated by the governing agency of the state in which they are physically operating. Your state will likely be different from this example and require a small amount of research and investigation on your part, but the similarities will be apparent. Illinois is governed by the Illinois Life Care Facilities Contract Act, from which the code of the same name authorizes oversight of CCRCs by the Illinois Department of Public Health (IDPH). IDPH regulates the residency agreements, called "Life Care contracts," monitors life care facilities, and ensures compliance with the act and code. This includes, but is not limited to, the required entrance fees, housing arrangements, personal nursing or medical care, and a variety of other services such as laundry, housekeeping, meal plans, and maintenance. Equally important, IDPH ensures all facilities must have an annual audited financial statement, and each must maintain an escrow account in the amount meeting or exceeding specifications set by the Department. IDPH will also regularly be present on site for an examination of anything deemed relevant to the CCRC's continued licensure.

For More Information

"About Continuing Care Retirement Communities: Learn What They Are and How They Work," AARP, accessed April 15, 2014

http://www.aarp.org/relationships/caregiving-resource-center/info-09-2010/ho_continuing_care_retirement_communities.html.

"What to Ask and Observe When Visiting Continuing Care Retirement Communities," AARP, accessed April 15, 2014

http://www.aarp.org/relationships/caregiving-resource-center/info-09-2010/ho_what_to_ask_retirement_communities.1.html.

"Continuing Care Retirement Communities Explained," SeniorHomes.com, accessed Nov. 30, 2014

http://www.seniorhomes.com/p/continuing-care-retirement-communities/.

"Contract Types: Continuing Care Retirement Communities (CCRCs) & Life Care Communities," ACTS Retirement Life Communities, accessed Nov. 30, 2014

http://www.actsretirement.org/retirement-resources/types-of-senior-living-communities/ccrc-contract-types/.

Jennifer Preston, "Faith-Based Housing That Meets Evolving Needs," NYTimes.com, March 12, 2014

http://www.nytimes.com/2014/03/13/business/retirementspecial/faith-based-housing-that-meets-evolving-needs.html?_r=0.

"Illinois Life Care Facilities Program, Life Care Program Update," Illinois Department of Public Health, July 2012

http://www.idph.state.il.us/about/lifecare.htm .

Alyssa Gerace, "Vi Residents Sue Over CCRC Entrance Fees," Senior Housing News, Feb. 23, 2014

http://www.seniorhousingnews.com/2014/02/23/vi-residents-sue-over-ccrc-entrance-fees/

Paula Span, "C.C.R.C. Residents Ask, 'Where's the Money?'" New York Times, March 20, 2014

http://www.newoldage.blogs.nytimes.com/?s=C.C.R.C.+Residents+Ask%2C+'Where's+the+Money%3F.

Alyssa Gerace, "New York Times: Vi CCRC Lawsuit Hinges on Lost Peace of Mind," Senior Housing News, March 20, 2014

http://seniorhousingnews.com/2014/03/20/n-y-times-vi-ccrc-lawsuit-hinges-on-lost-peace-of-mind/.

SECTION SEVEN

Touring Senior Communities

CHAPTER TWENTY-THREE

The First Visit

Whenever you anticipate beginning something new, especially when the venture has a critically important end goal, it's a good idea to learn as much as you can about the process, the players, and the cleanest route to benefits you're seeking. You need to know what's ahead, what you can expect, and any possible "tips" to maximize your outcome. That's exactly what we're going to do in this section and why I'm beginning with what is the biggest "tip" of all.

The power and control of the touring process—and to some extent, the tour's productivity—lies with you. You are the one who's really in charge of what you see, who you meet, and the impressions recorded. Depending on the flexibility and the goals of the manager touring you at the community, you may not always feel as though you're in control, but you are. You're in control all the way up to the worst that can happen—you become completely disillusioned and leave the community short of the tour's completion, decide that community's not going to work, and, still in control, you move on to visit the next community on your list.

You and the senior community's management and staff often come at the touring process from different directions, somewhat different points-of-view, and this is an unfortunate climate change in the senior-living industry during the last decade. Competition for new senior residents has become fiercer as the economy has limped along and failed to bounce back after banks ruined the housing market. Even though the personnel have their hearts in the right place and truly want to help seniors find good housing options, their message has been directed to seem as though their community is the only choice that is truly appropriate. That's foolish. There is no one place and only one place that will work to solve everyone's issues, but it does take the right place at the right time. Quite simply, that's why you're looking—to gather information—but be prepared for a manager who wants you to feel as though they, not you, are in control. With knowledge and careful planning, if or when you feel this shift, you'll be prepared to take back what's rightfully yours.

One of the biggest tools you can have for touring communities is a binder—or a place on your computer, laptop, iPad, or phone, or whatever works for you . . . just as long as it's something you'll use. This may sound too much like a school assignment, too organized, but you'll be thankful after touring several properties that everything you need has been categorized, tabbed, and is all in one place. Consider a separate tab for each senior community and a copy of the questions you want answered at each location. Also include bullet points of important topics to cover about your loved one (personality, health events, assistance needed, likes, dislikes). Be sure to have a page for all the people you meet at each community, both residents and professionals (with their titles). It's a good practice to ask for business cards. And it's your information: make notes! Your comments and notes will be an extension of a very important section, impressions. First impressions are lasting impressions, but you would be surprised at how one fades into another after an increased number of communities are visited. Your record can and probably should include all of your senses—smell, sight, hearing, touch, and taste—and with an exceptional tour, you'll want to remember all of it (good and bad). And most of all, how did you feel about the dialogue you had while you were there? How good was the communication? How well did they ask about your personal situation and, in turn, hear and process what you said?

Touring senior-living communities in the hope of finding a well-suited new "home" is a process, not a game of darts to see how close you can come to the target with just one throw. The process isn't difficult, but it is time-consuming and requires driving, getting in and out of the car, making plans, manipulating schedules, and meeting a lot of people. You ultimately want the result to be so satisfying that it's a pleasure to spend the money it will cost to live there, to organize the move, and to gladly do the cheerleading necessary to make the choice successful. The process begins with gathering information from a "first impression" at the community. It includes both calling for print materials you want mailed to you and visiting the community to gauge its "fit" for your needs. You can accomplish this one of two ways. Either approach can work, but depending on your immediate goals, patience, and tolerance for risk versus tiny steps in pursuit of a satisfying conclusion, one method will appeal to you more than the other.

The first approach takes planning after deciding which properties you want to tour:

Call each one individually and ask for the director of sales and marketing (prepare for a variety of titles, but you're looking for the manager responsible for move-ins to the community). If that person isn't available, you can accomplish this step with the receptionist who answers the phone. You want a full brochure mailed to your address (and not Aunt Jean's, unless you want a duplicate sent to her). Be sure to ask that all price sheets are included. The goal at this point is to get the information you want by being as stingy with your personal information as you want to be.

A phone call to the community will tell you a great deal about their operations. Are they staffed and trained adequately to appear ready to meet your needs, or are you transferred into voicemail or placed on hold? Is the person you seek present and ready to help? Do they ask for permission to ask you a few questions so they can customize the brochure's materials to fit your needs? Did they give you a cell phone and a direct call-back number to simplify reaching them?

If you give them your email address and phone number, you can expect emails and calls trying to get you come to the building and tour. On the other hand, if you want to look at the information first and decide afterwards whether or not to tour, then say that. You control the process.

There's a good chance that you won't get price pages unless you specifically ask for them. The trend is to not include prices, but the reasons have nothing to do with you and what you're trying to accomplish. They want an opportunity to buffer the cost surprise by showing you their beautiful, warm, caring community and telling you about what they can do to make the cost more palatable (for example, discussions about long-term care insurance or VA pension benefits).

The number-one goal of the community is to get you in their front door to tour because they want to control your first impression, put their best foot forward, and help you determine that you need to search no farther. If for whatever reason your goal is in alignment with theirs, then by all means go ahead and make an appointment to tour during your first phone call. If, on the other hand, you want to look at the materials to see if the community has what you need, whether you can afford to be a resident, or to organize your thoughts and questions, then stick to your guns and get the collateral materials first.

Assuming the materials you receive look like something you want to pursue, plan to call back for a tour time that's convenient for you. The additional choice you have to make at this point is whether or not your loved one attends the first visit with you. Their mobility, strength, attention span, and overall attitude are factors you need to think about. Since you really won't know how many good community options you ultimately have until after the first cut, it begs the question whether Aunt Jean needs to see all of the choices or only the ones that could work out well.

The other method of looking at communities is to just jump in and be spontaneous: you pass by a senior community and decide to stop and take a look at it. You decide to ask for a quick tour and some printed information, ask a few basic questions, and you'll be done with it in no time. Or maybe you plan to make a day of quick stops, check out several communities, and cross them off your list. This approach may especially appeal to you if you're in the midst of a crisis and must get Aunt Jean somewhere safe, quickly. You might also feel a surprise visit will catch them unaware and somehow prevent a cleanup designed to show off their community at its best. Chances are, however, each stop will take longer than you think, and there are a few disadvantages if you "drop in." The process could leave you wondering later if you gathered all the facts you needed.

You need to talk with the director of sales and marketing. That's who should answer your questions and show you the community. Equally important, you should be prepared to answer their questions about Aunt Jean and why you're looking at communities. The problem is that in today's world of senior living, the person you need is not going to be there about 50 percent of the time because they are required to market their services outside the building to the community at-large.

Your tour will still take place, but it will be handled by one of the other department managers (for instance, activities, dining, maintenance, or occasionally the executive director). Ask yourself if you're okay with the community's features, benefits, services, and the finer points regarding limitations on care being explained by the chef. Fingers crossed the executive director is available.

The reason it's important to spend your initial visit with the right director is the resulting quality of your first conversation, which is actually even more important than your first look around the building. You need to be asked the right questions in order to provide a clear picture of your situation, including your loved one's personality and abilities, what they can do for themselves, what they'll need assistance with throughout the day, and what is and isn't possible financially. The other department heads are likely very talented at their own positions and responsibilities, but they will very, very rarely get the full picture revealed. Why? Because even if they do a good job unearthing most of the information from you and showing you the community's highlights, their nerves fail them when it comes to asking about finances.

So what's the big deal? You just want a quick tour, right? The problem is, you don't want to spend your time chasing something that isn't going to work. Most of the time it fails on the finances. For instance, you need a property that will eventually take Medicaid when your aunt's money runs out, and this one doesn't have the ability to make the accommodation. Or, the current rent and care charges can be covered financially, but you're already at the maximum limit with no room or solutions for tomorrow's increases; you know this will mean another move in the near future. Or, the stumbling block may be a kosher diet, or the pet dog you swore would also make the move, or the crushed medications and feeding tube that are now a way of life. You need the right person to get the correct answers. You also need to meet the other professionals, such as the director of nursing, to confirm the necessary services can be met under the community's state license. These types of answers are exactly what the director of sales and marketing has been trained to provide.

The receptionist (or whatever director gives you the tour) will probably make note of any questions you may have after you tour the building, ask for your phone number, and offer to have the director of sales and marketing call you. This will most likely lead to either a long and complex phone conversation or another trip for you to the community to meet the people you need to meet and get the answers to your questions.

This section's theme now bears repeating: at the community level, you are the one who is in control. The owners-managers-staff are in business to make you and yours happy, to encourage you to see their community in its most positive light by making accommodations as necessary, because they need you. Without you and others in a similar position, they can't do business. They wouldn't have the money to operate. These communities pay all of their expenses—mortgage payments, salaries and benefits, food costs, lights, water, repairs, and much more—from their only source of income: monthly payments from the residents' assets. They need you! And there's real power in that.

If you don't like something or you feel like some features just don't "fit," tell them. You can be nice and, at the same time, honest. You have the potential to turn community features into something that better fits your needs, but you have to carefully select what's most important to you. It won't work if you paint yourself into a corner as a real pain in the neck who wants to manipulate everything. You need to pick your battles. There are many situations that won't require awkward discussions that can lead to a standoff: you simply ask if you can do something different, and though they may hem and haw a little, they will most likely acquiesce. Sure, you can paint the bedroom walls pink . . . and the rest of the apartment too, if it makes Mom happy. Yes, maintenance can order a tub-cut to turn the tub into a shower only. But after you assess what you most need to have changed and why, tell them, This is what I need. This is what I have to have to make this work. Make it clear it's a deal-breaker, and be prepared to walk if you can't get it. There may be nothing for you that rises to this level, but at least mentally walk yourself through the situation to be prepared if there is something you can't do without.

As you're shown the community for the first time, think in terms of what is already terrific and easily "sold" to your loved one, and what you wish you could alter a little to make it a perfect solution. Take a hard look at cleanliness, lighting, the condition of carpet, furniture and equipment (the community van, laundry rooms), and common space inside and outside (dining room, living room, TV room, sidewalks, and parking lots). How does the place smell? Are the halls long and the distance to common areas problematic, or is the layout senior-friendly? What are your initial impressions of the managers and employees; do they seem friendly, helpful, knowledgeable, and glad you're visiting? Are they fully present and enjoying what they do? How do they interact with the residents? Are the residents you see fully engaged in whatever it is they're doing, or do they seem bored, unattended, or (worst of all) sound asleep? And the litmus test: can you picture your loved one being happy in this environment?

After your initial tour is complete, be ready for a push from your tour guide to schedule a return visit with Aunt Jean—probably for a lunch or dinner tour, which is ultimately a good idea. This gives you and your aunt a chance to try the food, observe dining services and how meals are handled, meet more of the staff and some residents, and tour the community at large. However, it's the cart before the horse. They're assuming you love them and will be back; you need to talk with your aunt first and relay your impressions. Just be honest. You'll talk with Aunt Jean and call them if she wants to visit.

If the community will be scheduling nursing assistance for Aunt Jean to help with tasks that are difficult, then take control of the discussion about a return visit by asking what days are good for the nursing services director to perform Jean's healthcare assessment. By their state license, every potential resident has to have their individual assessment completed by the director of nursing—even though it may turn out the individual needs no assistance at this point—and coordination minimizes the number of trips to the community that might be necessary. Not only is completion of the assessment a requirement, but it is also the only true means of obtaining the total monthly costs of the community (rent plus personal care services), so why not combine it with the lunch tour?

After you walk out the community's front door, the first thing you do is make notes about everything you saw, thought, smelled, felt, and want more information about. What did you like? What was off-putting? Is this a keeper and a possibility, or can you not imagine encouraging anyone to check it out, much less someone you love? Remember, you're in control. The message goes through you to someone whose next chapter in life—and possibly, their last chapter—depends on your help and your interpretation of the facts. So do your best to get it right, interpret it accurately, and get ready for the next step.

When you call back to plan a return trip to communities that survive your initial scouting and become a destination for Aunt Jean to check out, go through what you want to see happen during your time there. If you want to enjoy a meal and have the nursing assessment completed, then be sure you let them know to make plans. If you want to eat lunch at a table with a few residents, of if you want to eat together as a family and be introduced to residents separately, then let them know what you want. If you want Aunt Jean to see only available one-bedroom apartments (which will be empty of decoration and furniture) during the tour or see only the model apartments (which will include a variety of sizes), then let them know ahead of time. This lets you customize a visit that fits your needs and lets the director of sales and marketing make the best use of your time together.

For More Information

"Do You Know the Top 5 Prospect Complaints?" Senior Living Smart, June 14, 2014

http://www.seniorlivingsmart.com/know-top-5-prospect-complaints/.

Amelia Willson, "5 Questions to Ask When Searching For Senior Care," SeniorAdvisor. com Blog, April 5, 2014

www.senioradvisor.com/blog/2014/04/5-questions-to-ask-when-searching-for-senior-care/

CHAPTER TWENTY-FOUR

Narrowing Options

Discussions have now taken place between you and your loved one about the community options you scouted on your own, giving you the opportunity to share what you saw and learned during your initial visit at one or more senior-living community. Hopefully the talks were productive and you've chosen to move forward together to tour the communities that survived the initial cut. A return visit with the potential resident is always a big day for individuals on both sides of the fence, and you should expect to experience an excellent presentation of the community. After all, when a lunch or dinner tour has been scheduled for a prospective resident and their family members, there shouldn't be a staff member in the building who doesn't know you're on your way. Whether or not you caught the community unaware on your first visit, this time you certainly did not. And the most important person, the individual you love and are trying to help find a new home, is in attendance this time.

A word of both caution and encouragement about your beloved prospect's behavior during this community visit: no matter what Aunt Jean blurts out that sounds rude or inappropriate, no matter how she behaves in a manner so unlike her normal behavior, don't let it worry you. Having been through countless first-time tours with seniors and their families, I can tell you honestly that any sales and marketing director helping you today, especially if they've been in the business for any length of time, has truly heard and seen it all over the years from the guest of honor. More than once a family member has charged into my office on the day of a lunch tour, late for the appointment, apologizing and explaining they can't get mom out of the car because she won't come inside. And they're completely frazzled because she sounded so positive when they talked earlier about the plans. They wonder, Should we just forget about it for today? Absolutely not!

You've constructed a plan, you've gotten her here, and she's just come down with a case of cold feet. If you were ever the new kid in school, if you ever had to walk into a classroom or a business or a new job, some place where everybody knew everybody else (or so you presumed), and nobody knew you, then you might relate a little to what's happening out in the car. Add to the mix that expectations are high, feelings are probably mixed at best that this is even a good idea, and it's no wonder that just going home (forever) seems like a pretty darned good idea right now.

The way I usually diffused this situation was to ask if I could go with the family member back out to the car, introduce myself to Aunt Jean, and let her know how glad I am to meet her and to have her see our community. I tell her I've really been looking forward to meeting her, but I get the feeling maybe she's not feeling the same right now. I give her every opportunity to chime in and talk to me, but my focus is on empathizing, recognizing that what she's about to do—meeting lots of new people, looking at a possible new place to live—is something that's really hard for lots of people. I assure her that our community is full of lots of great people I think she'll enjoy, but we're just going to get comfortable in my office first and get to know each other a little bit before we start looking around. Basically, I do the same reassurance beside the car that I normally do in the lobby: tell my guest how our time together will be spent, what's planned, how we'll talk first and get to know each other a little, what's for lunch, and then we'll take a look around, and ask if that sounds okay. In a beside-the-car episode, I've even told them if at any point anyone gets uncomfortable and wants to leave, that's okay, too. No one's ever left the building, and honesty beside the car has always worked to encourage a look inside.

The point is that whatever happens is okay. It's much more likely that whenever you take someone with you to a community to take a look around, they won't suddenly morph into a personality you don't recognize. There certainly could be few untruths that you overhear or exaggerations here and there, but it's honestly no big deal. I used to assure family members concerned about inaccuracies that my own parents were actors from way back: they could be in the midst of some debilitating health event and, when asked how they were doing, they'd say some convincing version of everything is fine. Sometimes to get to real facts or feelings, you have to carefully dig deeper to get to the truth, and that will happen over time. When a potential resident on a first tour is introduced to new people, a new place, a new concept for living somewhere they hadn't considered, and lots of choices, it takes some time for it all to settle in its rightful place. But it does eventually.

Once you're inside the community and sit together in the director's office, you can begin to observe something that's very important. Whether or not the community you're visiting is genuinely, deeply committed to a resident-centered philosophy is something that will show itself throughout the day is large and small ways, but it begins right in this office. Is your aunt the one who is being talked to directly, and is she the focus of the conversation? Is eye contact clearly being made with her? Is the conversation about her, or is she becoming the recipient of an "information dump" that's all about the community? You may or may not have had a thorough conversation and tour with this director prior to today, but you still know a lot more than your aunt does at this point, so this is her time. In fact, if she's not getting the focus she deserves, then catch the director's eye and unobtrusively do the head-bob-thing toward her so the point is made. You shouldn't have to do this, but nevertheless stay on the lookout for their focus throughout the day. There should be numerous small signs of respect, indications that caring for the residents and their feelings is what the job is all about.

If you have had the opportunity prior to today's visit to mention specifically what you want Aunt Jean to see and who you want to be sure she meets while she's in the community, then everything should be prearranged and unfold as you requested. If not, you'll have to take the bull by the horns before you leave the director's office. The day will be arranged in chunks of time—lunch, nursing assessment, looking at individual apartments, and getting a feel for the community at large—that will be arranged in an order that may or may not fit the your needs or your loved one's stamina (mental and physical), so jump in any time to curtail or redirect efforts. It's everyone's job to answer your wants and needs when you visit, but don't make them guess what those are.

Use what you know about Aunt Jean to make the day what it needs to be. If you know she has always been quietly private and loves to read on her Kindle or watch TV, then she's not going to need to hear about every activity to pull her out of her apartment and socialize; a copy of the monthly calendar will do the trick. Will she likely attend more entertainment and activities as a resident than you can imagine at present? It's a real possibility, but the benefits of socialization don't need to be a focus point unless that's one of your major goals. Similarly, if seeing only apartments that are fully renovated, empty, and ready to rent will make it difficult for her to imagine their appearance when full of her belongings, then ask to see the fully decorated model apartments before seeing available units. Even plans for completing the individual nursing assessment can be somewhat manipulated to fit your needs: you can't do away with the evaluation completely, but you can certainly reschedule it for another day and ask that the nurse come to Aunt Jean's home (or yours) to complete it. Yes, it must be completed by regulatory requirement, and yes, the nursing director would prefer to do it in her own office where she can continue to put out small fires with her staff as necessary. But, if Aunt Jean runs out of steam on her first day touring the community and wants to put it off until another time, it's probably a good idea. Tell them what you want.

Here's a word to the wise about apartments. You're looking for space that will make her happy and make your life easier because she's happy. Know the sweet spot: a big window with an attractive view that lets in plenty of sunny light; a spacious bathroom or big closets; a well-designed kitchen that makes baking cookies easy. Maybe it's not something about the apartment itself as much as its location within the building. If she's very social, she may want to be near the activity areas; if the apartment is small and she's a lover of books, then try for an apartment near the library. Whatever it is, mention it and firmly support finding it for her. Sometimes, if you've had a productive time on your own initial visit prior to today, you will have looked at available options and narrowed them in advance to only the apartments that fit the bill, but don't get proprietary about your selections. What you thought were the priorities can shift mid-tour, and she may like an apartment for unexpected reasons or for no reason at all. Don't question, simply rejoice. But, if she doesn't connect with any of the apartments, be okay with that as well; you can always return and take another look.

Here is the key, however: stamina allowing, be certain that you've seen all of the available apartments that you want to see. Some communities will insist they have only a very few apartments—say, four or five—available to rent, when in fact they have many more. This is done to create a sense of urgency and to make you feel as though you need to reserve a unit with a deposit today: secure that apartment before it's too late! It's entirely about their need (make a sale, boost the numbers), not yours, which should at a minimum tell you something interesting about their priorities. We all know the community setting is a business, but the focus can still remain on satisfying your needs at a variety of levels, which includes selecting the right apartment. They have only four or five apartments primed and ready for a quick move-in; at the same time, they probably have several that range from a real mess to almost done that may perfectly suit your needs, if you can look around the imperfections. If you suspect you're not getting the true picture about availability, feel free to question their total inventory of apartments.

CHAPTER TWENTY-FIVE

Closing the Deal

Let's say your day at the senior community with Aunt Jean has been incredibly productive, and you and your aunt have found exactly what you're looking for. The employees appear devoted, the residents seem happy, the food is great, the nursing evaluation is completed, and an apartment has been selected. In reality, this accomplishment will almost certainly take more than one trip in one day, but whenever it reaches this point, confirmation and simplification are the order of business.

Confirm your positive feelings by asking the director for names and phone numbers of resident family members you can call to inquire about their experiences with the community. A good selection includes both positive and negative views. Their negative opinions will likely have been resolved or tempered by interventions on the community's part, but the severity and length of the problem before resolution will tell you a great deal. Ask about specific departments or even individual managers, especially those who will be in close contact with your loved one. Open-ended questions return the most information: if you could change one thing about the community, what would it be? What is your loved one's biggest complaint about the community? Their favorite feature? How do you find the community's communication and response time to problems? Even this: Do the departments heads and directors return phone calls in a timely manner?

If you're investigating a senior community that is licensed by the state, confirm their verbal answers when you asked questions about the state's last visit and the results of their evaluation. Either ask at the community to see a copy of the state's most recent assessment or, for more anonymity, request information through the state regulatory agency. It's not that you doubt the truthfulness of their answers; it's just that you have a right to see the document for yourself and to understand expectations.

It's helpful to see the laws and how they translate into day-to-day performance measurements.

Simplify lease signing by asking for a copy of the lease to read ahead of time. You can either get a physical copy or request that a copy be emailed to you, whichever is more convenient for you. Leases can be quite long and dense, and you'll be glad to have made note of questions before the actual signing. Plus, it saves everyone a lot of time at the actual event by not having to go through it section by section, page by page. My personal experience has been with leases that were 25 pages and 110 pages, both for communities with independent living and assisted living; the length and specificity can vary greatly. The memory care lease ran more than 125 pages.

When you study the lease and the accompanying cost sheet(s), make note of line items that are problematic for you, either in understanding what they mean or in actually paying for them. What is the "community fee?" What does the second person fee (in the case of couples) cover, and why is it so much? I've been part of negotiations that resulted in serious reduction to the community fee, second person fee, and even monthly rent when the family pushed. Understand, though, that the decision is made above the community level and requires time in advance of the lease signing appointment. The negotiation is especially effective when the new resident is watching expenditures with the intent of being able to reside there as long as possible before assets are drained and a move to subsidized housing is necessary. If there's a problem with projected cost, see what you can do.

When you have put everything together and know the monthly cost for rent and services, the details of the services provided, and all of the extra promises that have been made to make the transition as easy as possible . . . if there is something missing, ask for it. If it will make things easier for you and yours, whether or not it's an actual deal-breaker in your mind, tell them what you need. Many times family members came to me with details of how difficult the actual move to our community was going to be for them to accomplish. Often there were siblings out of state, careers and kids' schedules to balance, or maybe family illnesses or other health events that were running concurrently with the preparation to move and the move itself. The additional logistics were more than they could handle.

Family members came to us with the same requests for referrals: did we know a good moving company that was respectful of Mom and her furniture but didn't cost a fortune? This was easy because we had an excellent mover we could recommend with full confidence. Then we started getting more and more requests for a professional organizer, someone who could help downsize the accumulation of collected treasures into a manageable amount of favorites that could be moved to the apartment. This could also include placing individual pieces with family members, resale shops or donation repositories, but they needed it handled by a professional with just the right touch to deal with stress and agitation.

We eliminated the repetitive questions and solved the bigger problem by creating our own program that could be offered to manage the move. In essence, we supplied a home-to-home move-in concierge service, which, between the licensed organizer, the local mover, and their crews, took most of the heavy work out of the transition. Best of all for the new resident, we paid for the package (minus extreme circumstances or "extras" the family wanted). The potential residents and their families loved it, and I considered it a profitable, one-time business expense that brought enormous good will and paid for itself with the first month's rent.

Finding a complete package like this one might not be possible, but you should ask how the community can help you accomplish the move. Decide whether you'll need financial assistance or manpower (or both), and tell them you need help making it happen. If you're honest and forthright, whatever answer comes your way will be helpful . . . if not with the task at hand, then at least by exposing the personalities, flexibility, and degree of willingness to advocate for the needs of their newest resident.

Any interaction with the community's managers, any answer to a question or request, will bring you more information than you suspected it would, as long as you're aware and looking at the bits and pieces that fall into your lap. You're gathering clues about how to deal with someone, how best to accomplish what you want or need, and where to find the shortcut to resolution. How you arrange the pieces and what you do with that information is for you to decide, but be persistent. Keep at it, and as always, I hope you find what you need.

CHAPTER TWENTY-SIX

Move-In Day

The big day has arrived and the move is ON! Today is the day that exploration—looking at options, exploring the possibilities in senior community living—becomes something very different. It becomes reality, and you're now a member of a new world order. No matter what your path has been to arrive at this point, you unknowingly share a great deal with others who have gone before you and found themselves, and their loved ones, at this very same juncture. You're exhausted, bone tired, but determined to accomplish what's on the docket for today. Nearly everyone who arrives where you are today feels the same as you do: mixed emotions, a sense of accomplishment, but so completely worn out.

Helping a much-loved senior transition to what will likely be their last home is a big undertaking, a job that's full of physical effort and mental gymnastics, one that's rife with emotional currents exposing feelings about what's happening today and, even more complicated, what happened years and years ago. Relationship history is a tricky thing. But through it all you've persevered and imposed order on countless pieces of the puzzle to arrive at this very moment, and it looks like everything will come together. Tonight, the newest community member will sleep in their new apartment.

There are as many ways to manage the logistics of settling your loved one in their new apartment as there are families trying to accomplish the feat. Everyone is trying to massage new surroundings into a familiar feel with beloved objects in just the right place, hoping that doing so will make the larger issue acceptable. This is great; it feels just like home, I'm sure I'll be happy here. Not to burst your bubble, but I've only heard that said once in many years, and the gal was sixty-five years old. The problem is that real comfort extends far beyond the apartment itself. This is a layman's explanation, but the level of comfort you're seeking is about one's body in space—the inside and outside of a person, both mental and physical adjustment—which generally takes a lot longer than one day. But a really well-executed first day is the beginning you need for a successful transition.

If your loved one is like the vast majority of new residents coping with their move-in day at a senior-living community—and granted there are some truly unique, seemingly ageless individuals (or ones like my sixty-five-year-old example) to whom this would be less critical—then there are a few guidelines that will make the transition easier. In the ideal world, most of the heavy lifting has been done prior to move-in day so that there's no remaining dilemma about bedroom furniture being too big for the room's dimensions or clothes not fitting in the closet. Arguments and guesswork need to take place before move-in day. Managers and employees at the community are accustomed to family members or friends coming in and out of the apartment and trying to do as much as possible ahead of time. Once the lease is signed, you'll have keys and can let yourself in and out. You can come and go as you please and make as many trips as is necessary to create a perfect, finished "look" to the new apartment.

I've seen family members leave before the bed is made and before anything is unpacked, arranged, or hung in the closet. One of the worst mistakes made on move-in day is to exhaust the new resident with effort to get the apartment habitable before nightfall; get it all done beforehand. Adjusting, in and of itself, plus the finality of the move is more than enough for one day. This is not like dropping off your son or daughter at college for the first time: they have all the energy in the world, are thrilled to be independent and in a new place, and want to put their stamp on every little thing to call it their own. Instead, your loved one is more than likely full of nostalgia, low on energy and strength, and longing for another place, another time.

The smoothest transition looks like this: furniture has been arranged, linens and supplies are properly stored, clothing and coats are hanging on hangers, beds are made, pictures and mirrors are hung on the walls, books are shelved, collections are arranged, and electronics are plugged in and operable. Everything's done. Even if your loved one has been a part-time participant in the process, there's a very valuable "wow" factor when it's completed ahead of time and they simply walk in to enjoy the new space. A vase of fresh flowers on the table never fails to broadcast today's a big day.

Beyond the apartment itself, there are several helpful pre-arrangements that can have a positive effect and familiarize everyone, but most especially the new resident, with some of the community's strongest attributes. Plan to make a memorable day of it; make it a fun event. If the community has a private dining room, reserve it for either lunch or dinner and plan to gather around the table for an enjoyable meal together. This creates a shared memory reminiscent of occasions in your history together. It's a spot of normalcy in their new home and goes a long way to disprove a common misconception belonging to seniors: everyone just wants to dump me here and nobody will ever visit me. This shows them there's still a place to gather, that they are what's truly important, and you'll follow them wherever they go.

If there's no private dining room or it's already booked, then by all means reserve a table to share a meal in the community dining room. While it's not as private, this has the advantage of getting the individual accustomed to space they'll use every day for all of their meals. Regardless of which location works for the shared dining, be sure to have one of the department managers or the host make introductions to key residents eating their meal at the same time. No one remembers all of the new names, but familiar faces click fairly quickly.

It's also a good idea to schedule time with the sales and marketing director to take the new resident and their guests on a casual walk around the community's gathering spots, public areas shared by the residents for activities, entertainment, socializing, or simply being in space other than their apartment. This works well either before or after the shared meal, doesn't need to take much time, and functions as a nice refresher course in where things are located. It's not uncommon for seniors to lose any sense of their bearings on move-in day and, at the worst of times, even to swear they've never seen the place before. If this happens to you and your loved one, don't panic; just grin and bear it. Don't push them by insisting they're wrong, they've been here before, and they loved it. Just take it as a sign of exhaustion and being completely overwhelmed. Even if you don't believe it at the moment, this too shall pass and everything will settle into a new normal.

Family members often stopped by my office on their way out of the building on move-in day, everything doable having been done, and the community's newest resident resting alone in their new "home." Inevitably there was almost a sense of wildness about their eyes, a barely controlled anxiety on their face, some people managing to mask concern better than the others. They were seeking reassurance that everything was going to be okay, that we would do the outstanding job we promised to do helping their loved one adjust to their new home. This is the point of letting go. Of course it's hard to "let go" because it involves trust, and it's about someone you love. And you're right; promises are easy to make, but trust has to be earned, so keep an eye on things, but from a distance. Feel free to call for updates. Whether it's a nursing or personal care question, a question about how well they're eating, or a question about whether or not they're attending what seemed like would be their favorite activity . . . if you want to know something, call.

Family would ask me, how long does it take for everything to become normal? To me, the dust just seemed to naturally settle after about three weeks. It doesn't happen overnight, but there's something about plus-or-minus three weeks that is almost magic. Patterns and schedules have taken hold. In the meantime, everyone at the community pays extra attention to the new residents and brings a lot of empathy to the equation: what they're accomplishing is really hard to do! I used to tell them that almost everything is indeed just a little different. If they're used to getting out of bed and turning right or turning left to go to the bathroom in the middle of the night, then it's probably going to be the opposite here. It's so confusing! The best message always is that everyone in their situation goes through the same adjustment period, and they, in particular, are doing a spectacular job. If that weren't 100 percent true, then after I completed the conversation with your loved one, you would be the very next call.

It's time to call it a day. Go home. Relax, then move into whatever routine calms you from a difficult day. As you peruse the day's events, try to look positively on what's transpired in the last twenty-four hours, the help you provided, the closure you feel about a difficult chapter finally coming to a close. It's okay to feel a tremendous mix of emotions at this point, but through it all, realize that a chapter has ended . . . and in all likelihood it would not have been as fluidly written without your efforts. You can sleep well tonight.

SECTION EIGHT

After the Bloom Fades

CHAPTER TWENTY-SEVEN

The Final Chapter

Each of you reading this book will have your own "final chapter" starring you and your loved one and differing completely from anyone else's. The twists and turns in content will be dependent upon the person you love and for whom you'll continue doing your best as their caregiver. In your weakest moments, it may seem they're the puppeteer and you're the hapless puppet, moving around as they command. But there's a very good chance they feel much the same as you do—not in control, participating in their own life as it unfolds. If they were truly in control, if they were using a pen to script the chapter on paper, would they allow it to be driven by their own physical and mental decline? No, I don't think so.

Yet as caregivers, we face the limitations and complications of what we're calling the "final chapter." It's loosely bound by bookends of time and measureable events: the completed assemblage of the place in which they chose to age and, hopefully much later in time, their final passing from this world. The time between the bookends, their last chapter and your last measure of time to share with them, is what will be unique, unlike anyone else's "final chapter."

As we move into our individual chapters, I believe our tendency is to relax and admire the neat, tidy arrangement of settled dust, much like your relief when things were "just right" after orchestrating changes to their home, everything designed to fit altered needs, abilities, and inabilities. It's a good thing to have that memory. I think it's also only human nature to want to stay in one spot, a comfortable spot, admiring the handiwork and being thankful when, in fact, little changes are probably taking place right in front of us. I'm not saying we become totally non-observant; everyday we're noting mood changes, eating habits, activity levels, supplies of all kinds, clean clothes, wants, needs, and the necessary delivery of assistance required to smooth the day. But the really big changes, the ones that can be life-altering, are often invisible to us as we go about handling the day-to-day needs of caregiving. The silent change-maker is often the chronic disease process residing within our loved one. For my mom, it was congestive heart failure.

There will always be acute medical conditions, like the falls and broken hips I've told you about, that will rear their ugly heads but eventually slip off the radar. Time passes, and if you're lucky, rehabilitation efforts take hold, and things pretty much return to the "normal" known prior to the crisis. If not, then the "final chapter" reads more like my dad's last years. My brothers and I were fortunate as regards those last years with Mom . . . her toughness was on full display, and her determination served her well. She ultimately returned "home" as she said she would— each and every time, until the last time.

Mom's congestive heart failure (diagnosed in 1994) was silently doing its thing over the years, quietly demanding more and more of her strength, and taking her into heart failure five times during her nine years without Dad beside her. In late August 2009, after fifteen years of bravely fighting this silent killer, Mom lost her battle and slipped quietly, peacefully away from us. This chapter is really her last chapter. It illustrates a number of twists and turns that you encounter along the way, how completely powerless you'll sometimes feel, and how you'll gladly take a breath and make whatever caregiving changes you can along the way. There were many problems to solve, many resolutions . . . and yes, each time I thought it was the last time we'd go through the process.

When Dad passed away in February 2000, Mom remained in the villa where they settled after their move from North Carolina. I thought maybe it would hold too many unhappy memories for her to stay there by herself, but the focus of her discontent was directed at the nursing home where he died and not the home they shared. She still had Schatzie to take care of, and that barky little Schnauzer proved to be worth her weight in gold. It was for Schatzie, who needed her breakfast and outside walk every morning (at the same time each day, according to Mom), that Mom even got out of bed. She was so full of grief after Dad's death that I hesitate to picture her days minus routine and responsibility.

Of course those same walks with the dog didn't work so well on below-zero winter days. The maintenance department kept the sidewalks and streets clear of snow, but the dog had to scout out her right "spot" by walking in the snow . . . then she'd raise a freezing paw and look mournfully at Mom. What's a mother to do? So she'd stick her cane from one hand in a snow drift and lean on it to temporarily balance, then—still holding the shortened leash in the other hand—lean over more toward "poor, shaking" Schatzie and rub the raised foot to warm it up! And Schatzie, who was no dummy, then raised another foot. And another. I fully expected to find Mom stuck in a snowdrift one day, having fallen while warming the dog's paws, but that never happened. Instead, the days grew longer and warmer, Spring arrived, and everyone's mood lifted slightly with more sunshine in the days.

Then Mom had her first episode of congestive heart failure. It was early in the morning and, of course, she was alone, but she followed procedure. She called the main building's front desk; they called an ambulance and sent a trained manager to stay with her until the emergency response team arrived to take her to the hospital. She progressed through the emergency room, then intensive care, then the cardiac unit, then the general hospital population, then the skilled nursing/therapy floor . . . altogether taking several weeks, and in the midst of it she received the sad news her pal Schatzie moved on to be with Dad.

During this time—and probably largely because of it—she agreed to move out of the villa and into her senior-living community's main building. By the time she was released to come home, we had duplicated the two-bedroom villa in a two-bedroom apartment on the first floor. We were focused on socialization, nutrition, and oversight for health concerns.

Mom's next health event was broken hip number one. After healing sufficiently from surgery, she rehabbed at the hospital and was released to her apartment too early; she needed a live-in caregiver for three or four weeks. Suffice it to say those were dark days . . . Mom hated the situation, behaved accordingly, and I recall multiple changes in caregivers. Some caregivers were okay, some were truly abysmal and replaced quickly, but they all nevertheless helped us bridge the time until Mom could fend for herself. We got through it.

Overall, however, Mom adjusted well to community living. She was eating better in the dining room, being slightly social, and always attending Bingo. It was actually at Bingo one afternoon that she had her second episode of heart failure; she just slumped over and put her head down on the table. But because she was surrounded by residents and managers, she was quickly tended to and in the emergency room in quick order. The same sequence as her prior heart event played out again: the emergency room, then intensive care, then the cardiac unit, then the general hospital population, and then the skilled nursing/therapy floor . . . altogether taking several weeks before she returned to her two-bedroom apartment and her pre-established routines.

My brothers and I were communicating fairly regularly about Mom's financial situation, which had appeared solid when she and Dad retired. Since Dad's passing, I was handling all of Mom's financial concerns, which mostly consisted of paying bills, but now I was also doing annual projections. With her small teacher's pension and Social Security coming in monthly, how long were the assets going to last? We started talking about options and, more specifically, about moving her to a one-bedroom in the community to save money. The two-bedroom had been the easiest, quickest solution to get her out of the villa and into a healthier environment, but it was pricey.

Mom admitted she didn't need or use all the space, so she was amenable to a move to save money with a one-bedroom—if and when one on her floor became available. We had tackled socialization, companionship, and oversight for health concerns, but now we were focused on making her money last as long as possible. We were on a waiting list, but it wasn't long before a one-bedroom (across the hall and three rooms down) became available. We made the move happen fairly painlessly with the help of local movers for the big pieces and my two brothers, my husband, and son. We insisted Mom not lift a finger except to direct us.

Still, the morning after her first night in the new apartment—which was in move-in shape with drapes hung, pictures up, closets tidy, towels and shower curtain up, all manner of knick-knacks appropriately placed, everything done—Mom was in heart failure. My brother, who was staying at our house, called Mom early, and she was so weak she could hardly speak. We quickly dialed the front desk to tell them to call the ambulance and send someone to be with her, and then we jumped in the car and sped to the community. Progress at the hospital was the same each time: entrance through the emergency room, then intensive care, then the cardiac unit, then the general hospital population, then the skilled nursing/therapy floor . . . altogether taking several weeks (and incredibly hard work on her part) before she returned to her one-bedroom apartment.

Each one of these heart failure events was very frightening, and every time there was a point (or two or three) when we thought we were going to lose her. But this one was really tough, and I particularly struggled with whether or not it was the product of the move itself. As someone who generally does not believe in coincidence, I felt the timing of the health event was pretty clear. And yet, we had made certain all she did was sit and tell us what went where. Beyond that, her job was to walk across the hall and three rooms down to view her completed new apartment full of her favorite things. Was I missing something? At this point I didn't know the term Relocation Stress Syndrome, but in hindsight, was that what had happened?

All in all, we were most grateful for my brother's odd feeling the morning of her heart failure, the little voice that told him to call several hours early "just to check" on her and plan the day. Without that, I'm sure she wouldn't have made it. But make it she did. I told you she was one, tough little cookie! She enjoyed her smaller apartment more than the bigger spaces she'd lived in. With a kitchen, living room, bedroom, and bath, it didn't feel "empty" to her with all of the unused space. And on the ground floor, it was one turn away from the door to a large, grassy inner courtyard with walkways and sturdy outdoor furniture in the shade. I was also able to plant a wrought-iron shepherd's hook with a finch feeder hanging right outside her living room window so she could see her favorite birds.

The next two years were blessedly uneventful, and we were very grateful. Mom was still coming over to our house every Sunday for dinner and a movie or television with the three of us. It was a practice started when Dad was alive but residing in a nursing home, and it seemed to mean so much to her that it became a part of her week and ours for almost ten years. Unless one of us was really sick, Sunday was inviolate. It was six hours of family life for her to be involved in each week, and if it felt good to us, then it felt even better to her.

The undercurrent during this time was still about money. She was headed toward qualifying financially for government aid and Medicaid, but I felt that solution was no solution as it would play out for her. At that time (2003–2005) there were no good community options near us for seniors with limited income and no assets (supportive living facilities), and the private pay community where she was living didn't take government aid. Minnesota, where one of my brothers lives, has a very strong set of community options, but a move out of state at that point in time would likely shatter her fragile grip on life. None of us were crazy about chipping in money every month to keep her afloat, but I really felt as though that's probably where we were headed.

Mom and I looked at a studio apartment in her building, a possibility to save several hundred dollars each month, but her reaction to it was disturbing. Her own mother had owned a studio apartment where she lived in Iowa for the better part of thirty years, first with Mom's step-dad and then alone after he passed away. Visiting Grandma every summer was our family vacation, and I remember countless phone calls, letters, and packages sent over the years in the hope of cheering up Grandma. I didn't realize until much later how Grandma's unhappiness took an emotional toll on Mom, the daughter. The thought of now living in a studio herself was swift and powerful. It wasn't something she could do.

Then I revisited an old idea that Dad had nixed before they even moved from North Carolina. There was another community a few miles from where Mom lived, and if her current one was "pricey" and a tad country club-ish, this one was several hundred dollars a month less expensive and much friendlier. We could secure a one-bedroom apartment there for almost the same price as the studio we'd recently viewed, and we'd push out the need for us "kids" to contribute financially for a couple more years. If she could only make the move and remain healthy!

Almost at the same time, I took a position at the new community as their sales and marketing manager, and there's no doubt this helped tremendously with Mom's feeling of security. However, we also did something very different with this move that made it much better for her. We told her we were "pros" now, and she didn't need to be involved at all, not even to the extent of telling us where things went. With the help of a mover, my husband, son, and my brother, it was actually very simple: a one-bedroom move to another one-bedroom with the same layout and only inches smaller.

On the day of the move, Mom had her hair done (including a perm, mainly to make it a longer appointment) and a deluxe manicure; then I took her out for a long, leisurely lunch at a cute little restaurant where we could linger. After I drove her to the new community and introduced her to a few of the key managers, we went upstairs to her new apartment . . . with some very sweaty guys still inside, but it was all done. She was amazed how much it looked like the apartment she just moved out of, and she loved her second-floor balcony looking out on a pond. A new finch feeder was mounted to her balcony railing, and she was good to go!

The new community became a very happy chapter for Mom and for us as well. She lived there a little over four years, and except for the bathroom fall and broken hip recounted earlier (pounding on the floor heard in the apartment below), they were years free of major health events. Yes, it helped that I worked there and kept an eye on her (fairly unobtrusively, I think). And yes, after about two years my brothers and I had to chip in financially to cover the monthly costs of her apartment, additional care, and medications. Was the money contribution painful? Yes, it was, but not impossible. We'd been able to put it off for a few years, and by the time we needed to contribute, she was ninety-three years old. Nobody from that generation planned financially to live that long, so I think we did a pretty good job stretching out every last penny. She remained in a community she liked, enjoyed companionship and activities to fit her needs, and was safely independent within the structure and oversight provided throughout the day.

Finally, however, she had a fourth episode of heart failure in August 2009, discovered by one of her favorite nurses who heard her coughing from the hall. She quickly diagnosed the problem, called the ambulance, and Mom was in the ER before she knew it. She gradually grew stronger day by day, and after about two weeks, she had progressed as far as the skilled nursing floor for some rehab. She was making progress but itching to get home. I visited her there one Sunday, and we talked about good rehab results meaning she could go home soon, maybe in a week or so.

She was unhappy to have been told her pureed diet would have to continue at home, and I assured her it could be done. No problem. I'd clean out her refrigerator and throw away some things that couldn't be pureed.

"Well, don't throw away the popcorn!" she said.

I asked, "And what are you going to do with that, puree it?" For some reason, that was hysterically funny, and we both got a terrible fit of the giggles. We'd just get straightened up, and then one of us would start laughing again. This went on for a while, and even as we were getting control of our giggling, we couldn't decide just what was so darned funny about pureed popcorn. But it was. We had a good laugh, hugged, told each other "I love you," giggled a little more, and promised each other we wouldn't eat too much pureed popcorn. I told her I'd see her in the morning, and then went home for dinner.

While we were eating, a doctor from the ER called: Mom was in heart failure and I was to go there immediately. She hadn't passed away, but she was struggling and they needed an interpretation on her Living Will. Several times in the past she had declined to sign a Do Not Resuscitate (DNR) order, but he was asking, "Did she want extraordinary measures taken to keep her alive?" It was confusing. Mom didn't want extraordinary measures taken to keep her alive, but the doctor was trying to resuscitate her . . . the right action with no DNR. Was he a confused Resident or Intern, or was I confused? It seemed to me the timing for decisions on "extraordinary measures" hadn't yet arrived, but was I doing the right thing?

That document, the Living Will, looks so black and white: don't do this, this, and this. By default, that means that, that, and that are okay. But you know what? Life is often somewhere in the gray, not in the black and white. It doesn't say when this happens, you can't do that. I just figured I couldn't tell the emergency team to stop trying with that cute, little mom who was in a fit of giggles with me just hours ago. When I got there, I walked straight back into the emergency room, and they were still working on her. They'd done chest compressions, used the paddles twice, and somehow there were no broken ribs. By her paperwork, I felt that was right.

It was a long night. They intubated her, then waited for her heart beat and blood pressure to get within the normal range and stay there. Hours later, we went up to the intensive care unit where she was hooked up to massive machinery and monitored by more machines. The nurses were immediately outside her door. I called my brothers, told them what had happened, and gave them the passwords to get information from the doctors and nurses. Off and on I dozed by her bedside, then sometime the next day went home for a quick shower. When I returned, Mom's doctor was waiting to talk with me.

The broad topic was hospice, but what touched me was how he shared bits of his personal life and his heartbreak in dealing with his own parents. The story had a point. Growing up in India, their dream for him was to become a doctor, and they paid for excellent schooling in the States so the dream, which was also his dream, could become reality. Now, many years later, their health was failing, and half a world away, he was of little help. The kind of medical facility he wanted to build where they lived couldn't be supported by the existing infrastructure; they couldn't come here because they could no longer make the long trip. Sometimes all of us, no matter how much we know or how hard we try, become powerless to help the ones we love most.

I said yes to the hospital's hospice unit on Mom's behalf. It was a homey, comfortable room with a private bathroom and shower, and the nurses took great care of her. She was off all of the tubes and machines, and she rested peacefully. They turned her regularly, kept her clean, bathed her daily, brushed her teeth, combed her hair, and without fail were kind and gentle. In the beginning there were regular intervals when she enjoyed a few spoons of flavored ice. Then it was a few ice chips, then nothing. The first few days, she had moments of cognizance, few and far between, but very clear. She knew who I was, where she was, and that there would be no more traumatic events. Then she no longer talked but would occasionally open her eyes, look around, find me, and go back to sleep.

The doctor intended on sending Mom back to her apartment after a few days of stabilization, but she became too weak to make the trip. I stayed with her, sleeping beside her in a chair that turned into a bed. I talked to her a lot: reminiscing; sharing memories, plans, hopes, and dreams, talking mostly about all of our times together as a family. I also eventually told her that, when she was ready, it was okay for her to go; I would miss her every single day, but that I'd be all right. She and Dad had raised us all to be strong, independent, well-educated adults, and we had loving families to support us. We'd be okay. I believe she knew what I said and that it broke my heart to say it. And I prayed, a lot. I prayed for guidance, and mercy, and forgiveness, and for anything else I could think of that might be helpful. I was shameless in my many requests. And then I talked to Dad, telling him he'd better on time to meet her because his was the first face she wanted to see.

It was a peaceful, gentle passing, and I will be forever grateful that Mom and I had that sad, sweet time together. It's now almost six years that separate us, and it's much like I told her it would be: I think about her every day. I miss her presence in my life, but I've also noticed I'm less emotional, less teary about the loss as years go by. Maybe it helps that Adam and I talk about them a lot, how we miss Sundays with Grandma, and how the smell of gasoline reminds him when Grandpa let him drive the golf cart when he was little. We now keep them alive in our hearts. I wish something similar for you.

The bookends holding together my "final chapter" must have been created with sturdy stuff; the content between them certainly grew long with twists, turns, and many frightful scares. But that's a good thing. That's life. Your "final chapter" will read differently, perhaps be shorter, or maybe even be longer. But when the chapter has been written, when the activity subsides and quiet surrounds you, I hope you know you were the best caregiver you could possibly be. I hope you have no regrets, you can listen to the quiet, and you'll call it Peace.